Simply 5

125 brilliantly flavored dishes
with 5 ingredients or less

WW Publishing Group

Managing Editor: Valeria Bloom

Food Editor: Eileen Runyan

Writer and Project Editor: Deborah Mintcheff

Contributing Editors: Lisa Chernick,
Leslie Fink, MS, RD

Nutrition Consultant: Laureen Jean Leyden

Recipe Developers: Terry Grieco Kenny,
Frank Melodia, Angela Nilsen

Creative Director: Ed Melnitsky

Design Director: Daniela A. Hritcu

Designers: Arlene Lappen, Rebecca Kollmer

Production Manager: Alan Biederman

Photo Director: Marybeth Dulany

Photographer: Jennifer Causey

Food Stylist: Rebecca Jurkevich

Prop Stylist: Bette Blau

Front cover:
The real deal fried rice, page 178

Back cover:
Plum crostata, page 187

**Soba noodle–
mushroom soup,
page 57**

About WW

WW (formerly Weight Watchers) is a global wellness company and the world's leading commercial weight-management program. We inspire millions of people to adopt healthy habits for real life. Through our engaging digital experience and face-to-face group workshops, members follow our livable and sustainable program that encompasses healthy eating, physical activity, and a helpful mindset. With more than five decades of experience in building communities and our deep expertise in behavioral science, we aim to deliver wellness for all. To learn more about the WW approach to healthy living, please visit WW.com. For more information about our global business, visit our corporate website at corporate.ww.com

**Lemony fennel
and radicchio,
page 137**

Contents

About our recipes, vi

Introduction, ix

Chapter 1
Rise and shine, 1

Chapter 2
Opening act, 25

Chapter 3
Big and small soups and salads, 49

Chapter 4
Main event, 81

Chapter 5
Eat your "greens," 121

Chapter 6
Beans, roots, and grains, 151

Chapter 7
Sweet nothings, 185

Recipes by SmartPoints® value, 198

Index, 202

About our recipes

While losing weight isn't only about what you eat, WW realizes the critical role it plays in your success and overall good health. That's why our philosophy is to offer great-tasting, easy recipes that are nutritious and enjoyable. Our recipes emphasize the kinds of healthy foods we love: lots of fresh fruits and vegetables, many of which are ZeroPoint™ foods that don't need to be tracked or measured. We also try to ensure that our recipes fall within the recommendations of the U.S. Dietary Guidelines for Americans—lower in saturated fat and sugar with plenty of fruits and vegetables, lean proteins, and low-fat dairy—so they support a diet that promotes health and reduces the risk for disease. If you have special dietary needs, consult with your healthcare professional for advice on what's best for you, then adapt these recipes to meet your specific nutritional needs.

Get started, keep going, and enjoy good nutrition

At WW, we believe that eating well makes life better, no matter where you are in your weight-loss journey. These tasty recipes are ideal, whether you're just getting started or have already reached your goals on the SmartPoints® system. Unlike other weight-loss programs, which focus solely on calories, the SmartPoints system guides you toward healthier foods that are lower in sugar and saturated fat, and higher in protein. But this isn't a diet—all food is in. Eating well should be fun, energizing, and delicious, so that healthy food choices become second nature. To get maximum satisfaction, keep the following in mind:

- On the *myWW*™ program—whether you're on Green, Blue, or Purple—eating a mix of foods (rather than all-ZeroPoint meals) can help keep you from feeling bored or deprived. Remember, there's room for all SmartPoints foods in your plan—variety is key to a healthy and livable eating style.

- The SmartPoints value is given for each recipe. The SmartPoints value for each ingredient is assigned based on its calories, saturated fat, sugar, and protein. The SmartPoints value for each ingredient is then added together and divided by the number of servings, and the result is rounded.

- Recipes include approximate nutritional information: They are analyzed for Calories (Cal), Total Fat, Saturated Fat (Sat Fat), Sodium (Sod), Total Carbohydrates (Total Carb), Sugar, Dietary Fiber (Fib), and Protein (Prot). The nutritional values are obtained from the WW database, which is maintained by registered dietitians.

- To boost flavor, we often include fresh herbs or a squeeze of citrus instead of increasing the salt. If you don't need to restrict your sodium intake, feel free to add a touch more salt.

- Look for these symbols throughout the book to choose recipes that fit best with your dietary needs:

  Vegetarian: Recipes that contain no animal-flesh foods or products made from animal flesh, though they may contain eggs and dairy products.

  Vegan: Recipes that contain no animal-flesh foods, eggs, dairy products, or honey.

  Gluten-free: Recipes that contain no wheat, barley, or rye, or any products that are made from these ingredients.

  Dairy-free: Recipes that contain no milk from any animal and no products made from animal milk.

  Nut-free: Recipes that contain no tree nuts or peanuts.

  Note: Recipes conform to the icon designations, but the headnote and tip serving suggestions may not.

- Recipe introductory headnote suggestions and tips ("Add this," "Try this," and "Serving idea") may increase the recipe's SmartPoints value; be sure to track any additional SmartPoints.

- For information about the WW plan, please visit WW.com/us/m/cms/plan-basics.

Calculations not what you expected?

The SmartPoints value for the recipes in this book is calculated without counting the ZeroPoint foods. However, the nutritional information does include the nutrient content of these ingredients. This means you may notice discrepancies with the SmartPoints value you calculate using the nutrition information provided for the recipe versus the SmartPoints value listed for the recipe. That's because the SmartPoints value for the recipes that contain ZeroPoint ingredients have been adjusted to reflect those ingredients, while the nutrition information provided includes the nutrition for all of the ingredients. For tracking purposes, use the SmartPoints value listed for the recipe. Also, please note, when fruits and veggies are liquefied or pureed (as in a smoothie), their nutrient content is incorporated into the recipe calculations. These nutrients can increase the SmartPoints.

Alcohol is included in our SmartPoints calculations. Because alcohol information is generally not included on nutrition labels, it's not an option you can include when using the handheld or online SmartPoints calculator or the WW app. But since we include the alcohol information that we get from our database in our recipes, you might notice discrepancies between the SmartPoints you see here in our recipes and the values you get using the calculator. The SmartPoints listed for our recipes are the most accurate.

Choosing ingredients

As you learn to eat more healthfully and add more wholesome foods to your meals, consider these:

- **Lean meats and poultry**
  Purchase lean meats and poultry, and trim them of all visible fat before cooking. When poultry is cooked with the skin on, you could remove the skin before eating to lower its fat content. Nutritional information for recipes that include meat, poultry, and fish is based on cooked skinless boneless portions (unless otherwise stated) with the fat trimmed.

- **Seafood**
  If you want to make sustainable choices, go to the Environmental Defense Fund at seafood.edf.org for more information and to download a guide, the Monterey Bay Aquarium at seafoodwatch.org, or the Safina Center at safinacenter.org.

- **Produce**
  In-season produce—at a local farmers' market, for example—is usually offered no more than a day or two after it's picked, so it's likely to stay fresher throughout the week than supermarket produce. Plus, shopping at a farmers' market is a great way to discover and try out new items you're not as familiar with. Also, stock up on produce like apples, beets, cabbage, carrots, celery, jicama, onions, potatoes, radishes, watermelon, and winter squash; these can last for weeks when properly stored and will give you ingredients to fall back on if you run out of more perishable items.

- **Whole grains**
  Explore your market for whole-grain products such as whole-wheat and whole-grain breads and pastas, brown rice, bulgur, barley, cornmeal, whole-wheat couscous, oats, farro, and quinoa to enjoy with your meals.

Warm roasted butternut squash salad, page 68

5-ingredient *myWW*™ recipes— easier, tastier, and faster than ever

Whether you are a family of four or five or a streamlined family of one or two, getting healthy, well-prepared meals on the table day after day can be a challenge. But we have the solution—recipes that use up to five ingredients and turn out tasty dishes.

Here's our secret: Our science-backed SmartPoints® system is at the core of each of our three plans—Green, Blue, and Purple—nudging you toward plenty of foods like fruits, vegetables, lean proteins, and healthy fats while guiding you away from foods high in sugar and unhealthy fats. No matter which plan you're on, you'll have a personalized amount of SmartPoints to spend on any food you love, along with 100+, 200+, or 300+ ZeroPoint™ foods that you don't have to measure or track. And when your ingredients are top-notch, there's no need to mask or muddle their flavor with unnecessary add-ons.

The recipes in *Simply 5* have been carefully crafted to highlight and showcase easy-to-find ingredients. Our plan when developing these recipes was simple: use only five ingredients (oil, nonstick spray, water, salt, and pepper are not counted) in a way that makes them shine. We've got you covered all year long, from breakfasts to soups and salads to main dishes and all manner of greens and grains. There's also a chapter on sweets, because they're simply delicious!

Although the recipes cut across the seasons, we recommend taking advantage of seasonal produce whenever possible. Not only do fruits and vegetables taste best in-season, they're also a better buy. Some of the tips suggest optional ingredients, such as an herb, spice, or other flavorful item that will contribute an additional layer of flavor. Take advantage of these suggestions when you have a few extra minutes to spend in the kitchen or already have the ingredient on hand.

So, what are you waiting for? Dive in and enjoy the *Simply 5* cookbook…. You have nothing to lose—and everything to gain when it comes to quick, good-for-you eating.

The minimalist kitchen

Even with recipes that use only five ingredients and require just a few pieces of equipment, if your kitchen is disorganized it will take more time to cook—and be less enjoyable, too. Take a hard look at how your kitchen is set up, then use our tips to turn your workspace around and make you a more efficient cook.

The kitchen set-up

Declutter and organize

- If you can't easily find what you need in your utensil drawer, consider buying a drawer separator to divide it into sections. Give away kitchen equipment you no longer use.

- If you have multiple sets of measuring cups or spoons or duplicate utensils, downsize to the number you actually use when cooking. Toss kitchen gadgets that seemed clever when you bought them—that garlic slicer or kale stem stripper—but now collect dust. Donate the excess to a local thrift shop or school.

- Park seldom-used equipment on a top shelf. If your kitchen space is limited, store items in another room or put them into covered plastic containers and store in your garage or basement. This is especially good for seasonal items such as Christmas cookie cutters, specialty cake pans, and very large pots.

- Make cooking more convenient. Many of the recipes in this book use only one pot, skillet, roasting pan, or baking sheet. Store the ones you use most often in a lower cabinet as close to the stove as possible. Put a nesting set of bowls and your cutting boards near where you prep. Place your go-to whisks, ladles, spatulas, and wooden spoons in a jar on your counter for easy reach. Keep knives safe and sharp by using a knife block or in-drawer slotted knife organizer.

Streamline your pantry

- Save space by eliminating tempting foods like cookies and chips to make room for healthier fare. The same goes for unwanted food gifts or condiments you thought you would like but didn't. Donate unwanted, unopened, unexpired items to a local food bank or give to friends or neighbors.

- Organize your pantry by zones. Store like things, such as canned broths, beans, tomatoes, salsas, rice, and whole grains together. Place frequently used items, such as oil, vinegar, pastas, and canned broths front and center on a shelf. Put items you use less often on upper or lower shelves.

- Put the dried herbs and spices you use most often along with salt and pepper in a basket, in a drawer, or on a shelf near your food prep area. You will be amazed at how much time this will save. Alphabetize the remaining herb and spice bottles to make them easy to spot. And while you're at it, toss dried herbs and spices you've had more than two years and only replenish those you use.

How to stock a basic healthy pantry

Keep these foods on hand and make cooking our five-ingredient dishes even easier and faster.

Pantry

- [ ] **Artichoke hearts, canned**
- [ ] **Bacon, fully cooked, ready to serve**
- [ ] **Baking potatoes, microwave-ready**
- [ ] **Beans, canned (assorted)**
- [ ] **Broth (chicken, beef, vegetable)**
- [ ] **Chopped nuts (assorted)**
- [ ] **Coconut, shredded**
- [ ] **Cranberry sauce, canned**
- [ ] **Dried bread crumbs (plain, seasoned)**
- [ ] **Green chiles, canned (mild)**
- [ ] **Instant espresso powder**
- [ ] **Grains, quick-cook packaged (farro, barley)**
- [ ] **Marinara/tomato sauce**
- [ ] **Pastes (tomato and anchovy), refrigerated upon opening**
- [ ] **Peanut butter**
- [ ] **Rice, boil-in-bag (white, brown)**
- [ ] **Rice, fully cooked (white, brown)**

Fridge

- [ ] **Baby lettuce, pre-washed (assorted)**
- [ ] **Baby spinach, bagged**
- [ ] **Beets, fully cooked, vacuum-packed**
- [ ] **Broccoli florets**
- [ ] **Brussels sprouts, shredded**
- [ ] **Butternut squash, peeled and diced**
- [ ] **Carrots, shredded or matchstick-cut**
- [ ] **Cauliflower crumbles (aka "cauliflower rice")**
- [ ] **Cheese, shredded and grated**
- [ ] **Chicken, rotisserie**
- [ ] **Coleslaw, broccoli slaw**
- [ ] **Edamame, shelled, fully-cooked**
- [ ] **Eggs, hard-cooked**
- [ ] **Garlic, chopped**
- [ ] **Garlic cloves, peeled**
- [ ] **Garlic, ginger, basil, lemongrass, and chile pastes, refrigerated**
- [ ] **Hummus**
- [ ] **Lentils, fully cooked, vacuum-packed**
- [ ] **Mushrooms, sliced**
- [ ] **Pesto, basil**

Freezer

- [ ] **Bell peppers, chopped**
- [ ] **Berries, unsweetened (various)**
- [ ] **Corn, kernels**
- [ ] **Edamame, shelled**
- [ ] **Mango, chunks, unsweetened**
- [ ] **Onion, chopped**
- [ ] **Pearl onions, peeled**
- [ ] **Pizza dough (plain, whole wheat)**
- [ ] **Spinach, chopped**
- [ ] **Waffles and pancakes (whole grain or whole wheat)**
- [ ] **Whole grains, fully cooked (farro, quinoa, wheat berries, rice)**

Global glossary

Travel no farther than your supermarket to enjoy these flavorful ingredients.

Bean thread noodles
These noodles are also called cellophane noodles, Chinese vermicelli, and glass noodles. Thin and translucent, they are made from mung bean starch. Bean thread noodles are cooked by being briefly soaked in very hot water until softened, then drained.

Chickpea flour
This flour is made from ground dried chickpeas. It is gluten-free, high in protein, and a staple ingredient in many cuisines. In Nice, France, it is turned into tasty pancakes known as socca that are enjoyed as a snack and cooked into a silky smooth soup (see recipe, page 50).

Chili-garlic sauce
Chili-garlic sauce is a spicy blend of coarsely ground fresh chiles, garlic, vinegar, and salt. It can be used as a condiment or added to cooked dishes, marinades, and sauces. Just a touch is enough to contribute bold flavor.

Chili oil
This vegetable oil has been infused with chile peppers that turn it a deep orange-red. It is a staple ingredient in Asian cooking and can often be found in the international aisle in supermarkets.

Coconut oil
Coconut oil is mechanically—not chemically—pressed from the meat of mature coconuts. It is solid at room temperature but quickly melts when heated. This oil is used in both sweet and savory dishes and is a favorite of vegans because of its rich flavor.

Crème fraîche
The term for "fresh cream" in French, crème fraiche is thickened heavy cream that is slightly tangy from the addition of buttermilk, sour cream, or plain yogurt. It is often used in place of whipped cream and is served alongside tarte tatin (upside-down apple tart), as well as soups and smoked salmon appetizers.

Fermented black beans,
Fermented black beans, also known as salted black beans, are made from black soybeans that have been salted and fermented, which gives them their rich, deep flavor. They are sold in small plastic bags in Asian markets and are inexpensive. Fermented black beans are usually briefly soaked in water then minced or mashed with a mortar and pestle before being added to stir-fries. A little goes a long way, so a tablespoon or two is all that is needed.

Fish sauce
Known as *nam pla* in Thailand and *nuoc mam* in Vietnam, this amber-colored fermented sauce adds rich complexity to dishes. The best-quality fish sauce contains only water, anchovies and salt. It is always used judiciously, so a bottle lasts a long time.

Hoisin sauce
This is a thick, dark sauce made from soybean paste, chiles, and salt and can also contain sugar, vinegar, and garlic. It is often added to Chinese barbecue sauces and glazes. Lee Kum Kee is a popular brand available in supermarkets.

Kecap manis
Used in Indonesian cooking, this is a type of soy sauce made by fermenting soybeans with salt and palm sugar. Star anise and garlic are also sometimes added for a more complex flavor. Kecap manis is thick and dark and reminiscent of molasses. It is best added sparingly.

Kimchee
Kimchee is a traditional Korean side dish. It is made from chile-laced Napa cabbage that has been fermented in crocks. It can be served on its own or added to fried rice or other dishes. It can be found in specialty-food stores, online, and in large supermarkets.

Lemongrass
This tropical plant is widely used in Asian cooking. It has a delicate citrus-floral flavor and is available fresh, frozen, as a fresh paste, and dried (not recommended). Look for firm, light green stalks, and

refrigerate tightly wrapped in plastic wrap for up to 2 weeks or in the freezer for up to 6 months. To prepare, cut off the dry end of the stalk and the papery top. Make a slit down the length of the stalk and peel off the tough outer layers to reach the pale, tender core. Smash it with the side of a large knife to release its oils and finely chop.

Mascarpone

A soft, creamy, mild triple cream–style Italian cheese, mascarpone is made from heavy cream. Sold in small containers in most supermarkets, it is best known as an ingredient in tiramisu.

Mirin

This sweet Japanese rice wine is used to lend a bit of acidity to dishes. Dry sherry and sweet Marsala wine make fine substitutes.

Miso

Miso is fermented soybean paste. There are three types: white, yellow, and red. White miso is made of soybeans and rice and is fermented for a short period of time, which makes it mild. It is best used in dressings, soups, and marinades. Yellow miso is made with fermented soybeans and barley, which lend it a stronger taste. It is best used in hearty dressings, soups, bold marinades, and glazes. Red

continues on next page

How to add a quick flavor boost
Let these exotics give a dash of wow to everyday dishes.

Aleppo pepper
(dried pepper flakes that offer heat, complex flavor, and bright acidity)
Store: up to 1 year in pantry
Try in: rubs, marinades, kebabs, grilled meat, pasta and rice dishes, sauces, stews, lentils, brownies, spiced nuts

Garam masala
(a mix of cardamom, cinnamon, cloves, coriander, cumin, black pepper, star anise, and turmeric)
Store: up to 1 year in pantry
Try in: rubs, marinades, curries, stews, braises

Harissa
(very hot seasoning paste from Tunisia sold in small cans and tubes)
Store: up to 1 year in refrigerator
Try in: marinades for grilled meat or fish, roasted vegetables, soups and stews, couscous, rice dishes

Horseradish
(member of mustard family, this root is prized for its ability to add a wallop of heat when freshly grated)
Store: bottled horseradish up to 2 months in refrigerator; fresh horseradish up to 2 weeks in crisper drawer
Try in: Bloody Mary mix, dips, beets, meat loaf

Sriracha
(hot sauce made from blend of chile peppers, vinegar, garlic, sugar, and salt)
Store: up to 1 year in refrigerator
Try in: any dish to add complex heat

Sumac
(slightly moist, coarse-grained dark powder with fruity, tangy aroma and slightly salty aftertaste)
Store: up to 1 year in pantry
Try in: potatoes, tomatoes, winter squash, onion, eggplant, zucchini, yogurt

Vadouvan
(French-style curry powder that contains shallots or onions; sweet with a touch of smokiness)
Store: up to 1 year in pantry
Try in: popcorn, dips, chocolate baked goods, vinaigrettes, rubs, marinades, vegetables, yogurt, grains, meat, chicken

miso, the saltiest variety, is made from soybeans and barley and is aged for a longer period of time. It is best used in braises and with vegetables.

Naan

A leavened flatbread from India, naan is made from flour, yogurt, salt, and yeast. Traditionally the dough is slapped against the wall of a tandoor oven until flattened then baked over a wood fire. It is best enjoyed brushed with ghee (clarified butter). Stonefire Authentic Flatbreads is a brand of naan available in supermarkets.

Oyster sauce

Oyster sauce is a rich concentrated blend of oyster, soy sauce, sugar, and salt that is thickened with cornstarch. This brown sauce is strongly flavored so is best used sparingly in cooked dishes such as stir-fries. It is commonly used in Cantonese, Thai, and Vietnamese cooking.

Pancetta

This Italian-style bacon is salt cured but not smoked. It is found in specialty food stores where it is sliced to order. You can also find it diced in small containers alongside the pre-sliced cold cuts.

Parmigiano-Reggiano

The only authentic Parmesan cheese is Parmigiano-Reggiano. It is made from cow's milk and is aged for at least 2 years in specially designated areas in Italy. It has a rich, sharp flavor and a creamy, granular texture. Look for a yellow rind with the words Parmigiano-Reggiano stamped. Refrigerate double-wrapped in wax paper and a zip-close plastic bag to keep it fresh.

Pecorino-Romano

This is a hard, pungent sheep's milk cheese from Italy. Due to its saltier nature, it should be added judiciously to dishes where a bit of salty, cheesy punch is a welcome addition.

Pepperoncini

These brined sweet peppers are medium hot. They make a great addition to sandwiches, antipasto platters, and Greek salads.

Prosciutto

An Italian dry-cured ham, prosciutto is served very thinly sliced. It has a sweet, meaty, buttery flavor and is produced in several regions in Italy. Prosciutto di Parma is the mildest and sweetest variety of prosciutto and is a bit pricier. Prosciutto is sold in specialty food stores, where it is sliced to order and pre-sliced in supermarkets.

Rice stick noodles

These noodles are made from rice flour and water. They are available in thin, medium, and wide widths. Rice noodles are cooked in boiling water until softened before being added to dishes. Wide rice noodles are best known for their use in pad thai, a noodle dish from Thailand.

Ricotta salata

This cheese is made from ricotta cheese. Ricotta means "re-cooked" and salata means "salted." To make ricotta salata, fresh ricotta cheese is pressed, salted, and aged for a minimum of 90 days. Ricotta salata, which resembles feta cheese, is most often used in salads and is ideal for shredding and slicing.

Sambal oelek

This Indonesian ground chile paste is used to add pure heat to dishes. One of the most popular brands in the U.S. is Huy Fong Foods, the California-based company that also produces Sriracha.

Thai curry paste

Thai curry paste is available both red and green. Green curry paste, which is quite hot, is made from a mix of green chiles, lemongrass, garlic, shrimp paste, kaffir lime leaves, and salt. Red curry paste is a blend of red chiles and spices and has a medium level of heat.

Tomato and
garlic–stuffed
peppers, page 144

Chapter 1
Rise and shine

Gruyère and asparagus frittata, 3

Overstuffed Western omelette, 4

Broccoli-egg strudel, 5

Zucchini and goat cheese omelette, 7

Baked eggs in tomatoes Florentine, 8

Greek-style breakfast pitas, 11

Skinny breakfast sausages and eggs, 12

Bacon and cheddar–coddled eggs, 13

Cheddar grits with bacon and kale, 14

Chilaquiles bake, 16

Savory steel-cut oats with kale, 17

Tropical oats with chia seeds, 18

Maple breakfast pudding, 20

Polenta with brown-sugar ricotta, 21

Red, white, and blue parfaits, 23

Gruyère and asparagus frittata

Gruyère and asparagus frittata

Serves 4

Buttery, nutty Gruyère is the perfect partner for the asparagus in this elegant yet easy frittata. This delectable cheese gets its name from a valley in Switzerland.

2	tsp olive oil
10	asparagus spears, trimmed and cut into 1-inch pieces
1	large shallot, minced
5	large eggs
1	tbsp water
½	tsp salt
¼	tsp black pepper
¼	cup shredded Gruyère or Swiss cheese

1 Preheat broiler.

2 In a 10-inch ovenproof skillet over medium-high heat, warm oil. Add asparagus and shallot and cook, stirring frequently, until vegetables have softened, about 4 minutes.

3 Meanwhile, in a medium bowl, beat eggs, water, salt, and pepper; stir in Gruyère. Pour egg mixture over asparagus, gently stirring until combined. Reduce heat to medium and cook, covered, until eggs have set in the center, about 5 minutes.

4 Place frittata under broiler, 5 inches from heat source, and broil until lightly browned, about 1 minute. Let frittata stand about 2 minutes before cutting into wedges.

Per serving (¼ of frittata): 185 Cal, 13 g Total Fat, 5 g Sat Fat, 482 mg Sod, 4 g Total Carb, 2 g Sugar, 1 g Fib, 13 g Prot.

Overstuffed Western omelette

Serves 2

Brimming with onion, bell pepper, and diced ham, this diner egg dish is also called a Denver omelette. Unlike the classic French version, where the filling is enclosed in the eggs, here they're poured over the filling and it all gets cooked together.

2	tsp canola oil
½	cup diced red bell pepper
½	cup diced green bell pepper
2	scallions, thinly sliced
¼	lb low-sodium ham, diced
¼	tsp salt
⅛	tsp black pepper
4	large eggs, lightly beaten

1 In a medium nonstick skillet over medium heat, warm oil. Add bell peppers, scallions, ham, salt, and black pepper and cook, stirring, until vegetables have softened, about 5 minutes.

2 Pour eggs over vegetable mixture and cook until eggs are almost set, about 2 minutes. Use a silicone spatula to gently lift edge of eggs to allow uncooked portion to run underneath. Fold omelette in half and cook until set, about 1 minute longer. Cut omelette in half and place one portion on each of 2 plates.

Per serving (½ of omelette): 285 Cal, 17 g Total Fat, 4 g Sat Fat, 979 mg Sod, 6 g Total Carb, 2 g Sugar, 2 g Fib, 25 g Prot.

Add this
Our Western omelette is a classic, but to make it heartier, add ½ cup packaged diced cooked potatoes (found in the produce section of supermarkets) to the skillet along with the bell peppers in step 1.

Broccoli-egg strudel

Serves 6

Nonstick spray

2   cups small broccoli florets

10 (9 x 14-inch) sheets phyllo
    dough, thawed if frozen

4   large eggs

½   tsp salt

¼   tsp black pepper

2   tsp olive oil

½   cup shredded reduced-fat
    Jarlsberg cheese

1 Preheat oven to 375°F. Spray a rimmed baking sheet with nonstick spray.

2 Meanwhile, bring a medium saucepan of water to a boil. Add broccoli and cook until crisp-tender, about 3 minutes. Drain and pat dry with paper towels. Set aside.

3 Lay 1 phyllo sheet on work surface, with long side facing you. (Keep remaining dough covered with a damp kitchen towel and plastic wrap to prevent it from drying out.) Lightly spray phyllo with nonstick spray. Layer 9 more phyllo sheets on top, lightly spraying each sheet. Cover with plastic wrap.

4 In a medium bowl, beat eggs, salt, and pepper. Stir in broccoli.

5 In medium nonstick skillet over medium heat, warm oil. Add egg mixture and cook, stirring with a silicone spatula, until just set, about 2 minutes. Spoon broccoli-egg mixture over phyllo, leaving a 2-inch border. Sprinkle with Jarlsberg.

6 Fold short sides of phyllo over filling, then gently roll up jelly-roll style. Place strudel, seam-side down, on prepared baking sheet and lightly spray with nonstick spray. Cut 4 (1-inch) slits in top of strudel to allow steam to escape. Bake until filling is heated through and phyllo is golden, about 20 minutes. Let strudel cool on baking sheet on a wire rack 15 minutes. Cut into 6 slices.

Per serving (1 slice): 185 Cal, 8 g Total Fat, 2 g Sat Fat, 485 mg Sod, 19 g Total Carb, 1 g Sugar, 1 g Fib, 9 g Prot.

**Zucchini and
goat cheese
omelette**

Zucchini and goat cheese omelette

Serves 1

2	tsp olive oil, divided
1	small zucchini, cut into matchstick strips
2	large egg whites
1	large egg
¼	tsp salt
⅛	tsp black pepper
2	tbsp crumbled soft goat cheese
4	basil leaves, thinly sliced

1 In a small nonstick skillet over medium heat, warm 1 tsp oil. Add zucchini and cook, stirring, until crisp-tender, about 2 minutes. Transfer to a small bowl and set aside.

2 In another small bowl, whisk together egg whites, egg, salt, and pepper.

3 In the same skillet (no need to wash it) over medium heat, warm remaining 1 tsp oil. Pour egg mixture into skillet and tilt so eggs cover bottom of skillet. Cook, without stirring, until bottom of egg mixture is almost set, about 2 minutes.

4 Spoon zucchini onto half of eggs and sprinkle with goat cheese and basil. Fold unfilled portion of eggs over filling to enclose. Cook until omelette is set, about 1 minute longer.

Per serving (1 omelette): 287 Cal, 21 g Total Fat, 7 g Sat Fat, 911 mg Sod, 5 g Total Carb, 4 g Sugar, 1 g Fib, 21 g Prot.

Baked eggs in tomatoes Florentine

Serves 4

The most efficient way to hollow out a tomato is with a grapefruit knife. It has an angled tip and a blade that is serrated on both sides.

4	(½-lb) ripe tomatoes
½	tsp salt, divided
2	tbsp grated Parmesan
1	tbsp Italian-seasoned dried bread crumbs
2	tsp olive oil
1	(5-oz) container baby spinach
¼	tsp black pepper, plus more for serving
4	large eggs

Large pinch coarse sea salt, such as Maldon

1 Preheat oven to 400°F. Line a medium baking sheet with parchment paper.

2 Meanwhile, with a small serrated knife, cut ½-inch slice off top of each tomato and discard. With a grapefruit knife or same serrated knife, carefully cut around inside of each tomato to remove fleshy center. With a spoon, scoop out juicy pulp with seeds and press through a small sieve set over cup. Measure out ¼ cup tomato water and reserve. Discard any remaining tomato water and seeds. Sprinkle tomato shells with ¼ tsp salt.

3 In a cup, mix together Parmesan and bread crumbs.

4 In a large skillet over medium heat, warm oil. Add spinach, remaining ¼ tsp salt, ¼ tsp pepper, and reserved tomato water. Cook, stirring, until spinach is wilted and tomato water has evaporated, about 3 minutes. Stir in Parmesan-crumb mixture.

5 Place tomatoes on prepared baking sheet and bake 6 minutes. Spoon spinach mixture into tomatoes, dividing evenly. Use back of spoon to line tomato shells with spinach, leaving centers empty. Crack 1 egg into a cup, then a slip into 1 tomato. Repeat with remaining tomatoes.

6 Cover tomatoes with a sheet of nonstick foil and bake 10 minutes. Uncover and bake until tomatoes are tender, egg whites have set, and yolks are slightly runny, about 10 minutes more. Sprinkle pepper and sea salt over each egg and serve.

Per serving (1 stuffed tomato): 161 Cal, 9 g Total Fat, 2 g Sat Fat, 543 mg Sod, 12 g Total Carb, 6 g Sugar, 4 g Fib, 10 g Prot.

Baked eggs in
tomatoes Florentine

**Greek-style
breakfast pitas**

Greek-style breakfast pitas

Serves 2

Not planning a trip to Greece anytime soon? Don't despair. Enjoy some typical Greek ingredients by whipping up this easy breakfast pita sandwich. Add ¼ tsp dried Greek seasoning and 2 to 3 tsp chopped fresh oregano, if you'd like.

Nonstick spray

3   large eggs

¼   cup crumbled reduced-fat
     feta

¼   tsp black pepper

⅛   tsp salt

1   cup tightly packed
     baby spinach

½   cup grape or cherry
     tomatoes, halved

1   large whole-wheat pita
     bread, halved and toasted

1 In a small bowl, beat eggs. Stir in feta, pepper, and salt.

2 Spray a medium heavy skillet with nonstick spray and set over medium-high heat. Add spinach and cook, stirring occasionally, until wilted, about 2 minutes.

3 Reduce heat to medium. Add egg mixture and tomatoes and cook, stirring frequently, until eggs are just set, about 1½ minutes. Spoon egg-tomato mixture evenly into pita halves.

Per serving (¾ cup egg mixture and ½ pita): 226 Cal, 10 g Total Fat, 4 g Sat Fat, 600 mg Sod, 19 g Total Carb, 2 g Sugar, 3 g Fib, 16 g Prot.

Skinny breakfast sausages and eggs

Serves 4

Nonstick spray

½ **lb ground turkey (7% fat or less)**

2 **to 3 tsp finely chopped sage (or 1 tsp dried)**

1 **tsp finely chopped thyme**

¼ **tsp salt (or to taste)**

¼ **tsp black pepper**

4 **large eggs, poached, scrambled, or fried**

1 In a large bowl, combine turkey, sage, thyme, salt, and pepper. Using a fork, gently mix until seasonings are evenly incorporated but not overmixed.

2 Place a sheet of parchment paper or nonstick foil on work surface. Divide turkey mixture into 8 equal portions and place on parchment, using about 2 tbsp turkey mixture for each. With damp hands, shape into 2½-inch round patties (don't worry if edges look craggy or have cracks).

3 Generously spray a large nonstick skillet with nonstick spray and set over medium heat. Place patties in skillet and cook until sausages are lightly browned and just cooked through, about 2 minutes per side. Serve with eggs of choice.

Per serving (2 sausage patties and 1 egg): 160 Cal, 10 g Total Fat, 3 g Sat Fat, 256 mg Sod, 1 g Total Carb, 0 g Sugar, 0 g Fib, 17 g Prot.

Bacon and cheddar–coddled eggs

Serves 4

Wouldn't recognize coddled eggs if you saw them? They're simply eggs cooked gently in custard cups or lidded ceramic coddling cups, usually in a hot-water bath. Brits love their coddled eggs served with crisp toast "fingers" for dunking into the yolks.

Nonstick spray

½   **cup frozen chopped spinach, thawed and squeezed dry**

4   **large eggs**

¼   **tsp black pepper**

⅛   **tsp salt**

4   **slices packaged fully cooked bacon, broken into pieces or chopped**

¼   **cup shredded reduced-fat cheddar or Swiss cheese**

1   Preheat oven to 350°F. Spray 4 (8-oz) custard cups or ramekins with nonstick spray; place on a small rimmed baking sheet.

2   Divide spinach evenly among prepared custard cups. In a medium bowl, beat eggs, pepper, and salt; pour into cups, dividing evenly. Top with bacon and sprinkle each with 1 tbsp cheddar. Bake until eggs are just set, about 20 minutes.

Per serving (1 coddled egg): 165 Cal, 11 g Total Fat, 5 g Sat Fat, 403 mg Sod, 2 g Total Carb, 0 g Sugar, 1 g Fib, 14 g Prot.

Cheddar grits with bacon and kale

Serves 4

The key to creamy, lump-free grits is slowly adding the grits while constantly whisking. Once all the grits have been added, it's just a matter of cooking them until they're thickened.

Olive-oil nonstick spray

4	**cups water**
1	**cup quick-cooking grits**
3	**cups lightly packed torn kale**
2	**tsp Cajun seasoning**
¼	**tsp salt**
4	**(¾-oz) slices Canadian bacon, diced**
½	**cup shredded reduced-fat cheddar**

1 In a medium saucepan, bring water to a boil. Slowly whisk in grits. Reduce heat to medium-low and cook, stirring occasionally, until grits have thickened, about 5 minutes. Remove saucepan from heat and cover to keep warm.

2 Meanwhile, warm a large skillet over medium-high heat. Add kale and spray with nonstick spray, tossing until coated. Cook, stirring frequently, until kale is wilted and any liquid has evaporated, about 2 minutes. Stir in Cajun seasoning and salt.

3 Push kale to one side of pan. Add Canadian bacon and cook, stirring once or twice, until heated through, about 1 minute.

4 Spoon grits evenly into 4 bowls. Top evenly with kale-bacon mixture and sprinkle each with 2 tbsp cheddar.

Per serving (1¼ cups): 260 Cal, 7g Total Fat, 4 g Sat Fat, 1,110 mg Sod, 33 g Total Carb, 1 g Sugar, 2 g Fib, 15 g Prot.

Serving idea
Start your meal with a fresh citrus salad of grapefruit and orange segments, sprinkled with thinly sliced mint and pomegranate arils, which can be found fresh or frozen.

Cheddar grits with bacon and kale

Chilaquiles bake

Serves 4

This classic Mexican dish is comfort food at its best and a great way to use up leftover tortillas. To make it even tastier, chilaquiles is usually served with a side of refried beans or diced nopalitos (cactus leaves).

Nonstick spray

⅓ **cup canned black beans, rinsed and drained**

1 **(6-inch) corn tortilla, cut in half and then crosswise into thin strips**

⅓ **cup shredded reduced-fat Pepper Jack cheese**

6 **large eggs**

⅓ **cup fat-free salsa verde, plus ¼ cup for serving**

1 Preheat oven to 350°F. Spray 4 (6-oz) custard cups or ramekins with nonstick spray.

2 Among prepared cups, evenly divide beans, tortilla strips, and Pepper Jack cheese. In a medium bowl, lightly beat eggs. Stir in ⅓ cup of salsa. Pour egg mixture evenly into cups and place on a small rimmed baking sheet. Bake until eggs are just set in center, about 30 minutes. Serve with remaining ¼ cup salsa.

Per serving (1 custard cup): 180 Cal, 9 g Total Fat, 4 g Sat Fat, 414 mg Sod, 10 g Total Carb, 2 g Sugar, 2 g Fib, 14 g Prot.

Try this
Make this classic Tex-Mex breakfast dish even more delish by topping each serving with a 2-tbsp dollop of light sour cream. While you're at it, sprinkle the dish with chopped cilantro and thinly sliced jalapeño rings.

Savory steel-cut oats with kale

Serves 4

We used Quaker oats in this recipe. If you use a different brand, keep in mind that the amount of water and the cooking time may be different than what is stated below.

Olive-oil nonstick spray

4   scallions, sliced

1   garlic clove, thinly sliced

1   cup steel-cut oats

3   cups water

¾   tsp salt

1   cup frozen chopped kale, thawed

¼   tsp black pepper

4   slices turkey bacon, crisp-cooked and torn into small pieces

1 Spray a medium saucepan with nonstick spray and set over medium heat. Add scallions and garlic and cook, stirring occasionally, until softened, about 3 minutes.

2 Add oats, water, and salt to scallion mixture and bring to a boil. Reduce heat and simmer, covered, 15 minutes. Stir in kale and pepper and cook, covered, until oats have softened and most of water is absorbed, about 15 minutes more.

3 Among four bowls, evenly divide oat mixture and sprinkle with bacon.

Per serving (1 cup oat mixture and 1 slice bacon): 194 Cal, 5 g Total Fat, 1 g Sat Fat, 612 mg Sod, 30 g Total Carb, 1 g Sugar, 5 g Fib, 8 g Prot.

Serving idea
Feeling extra hungry? You can top each serving of oats with a poached egg, and maybe a few shakes of your favorite hot sauce.

Tropical oats with chia seeds

Serves 4

In this tropics-inspired dish, coconut water infuses subtle flavor into the oatmeal. Each serving is topped with juicy pineapple pieces and crisp coconut chips. Chia seeds, on-trend and good for you, make an appearance as well.

2 **cups pure coconut water**

1 **cup quick-cooking oats**

2 **tbsp chia seeds**

2 **cups diced pineapple or kiwi**

¼ **cup toasted sweetened coconut chips**

1 In a medium saucepan, bring coconut water to a boil; add oats and chia seeds. Reduce heat and simmer, stirring occasionally, until oats are cooked and mixture has thickened, about 5 minutes.

2 Into 4 bowls, evenly spoon oat mixture. Top evenly with fruit and coconut chips.

Per serving (½ cup oat mixture, ½ cup fruit, and 1 tbsp coconut):
186 Cal, 5 g Total Fat, 2 g Sat Fat, 136 mg Sod, 33 g Total Carb, 13 g Sugar, 7 g Fib, 5 g Prot.

**Tropical oats
with chia seeds**

Maple breakfast pudding

Serves 4

How about serving a steaming frothy cappuccino sprinkled with ground cinnamon alongside this luscious morning meal? An 8-oz cappuccino prepared with fat-free milk is guaranteed to get your day off to a good start.

2½ **cups plain unsweetened soy milk**

¾ **cup long-grain brown rice**

¼ **cup raisins or dried cranberries**

1 **tbsp maple syrup**

¾ **tsp ground cinnamon**

¼ **tsp salt**

1 In a medium saucepan over medium-high heat, bring soy milk to a boil. Stir in rice, raisins, maple syrup, cinnamon, and salt. Return to a boil. Reduce heat to low and cook, covered, until rice is tender and milk is almost absorbed, about 45 minutes.

2 Remove saucepan from heat and let stand 10 minutes before serving.

Per serving (⅔ cup): 223 Cal, 4 g Total Fat, 1 g Sat Fat, 207 mg Sod, 40 g Total Carb, 9 g Sugar, 3 g Fib, 8 g Prot.

Polenta with brown-sugar ricotta

Serves 4

Instant polenta is what makes this recipe a snap to prepare. Even though it cooks in just minutes, the polenta is still a whole grain and a great way to start your day right.

1	**cup low-fat (1%) milk**
1	**cup water**
⅛	**tsp salt**
⅔	**cup part-skim ricotta**
1	**tbsp light brown sugar**
½	**tsp vanilla extract**
½	**cup instant polenta**

1 In a medium saucepan, combine milk, water, and salt. Bring to a boil over medium-high heat.

2 Meanwhile, in a food processor, combine ricotta, brown sugar, and vanilla and process until smooth. Set aside.

3 To milk-water mixture, slowly add polenta in a thin, steady stream, whisking constantly. Cook, stirring constantly, until polenta has thickened and is creamy, 3 to 5 minutes. Divide polenta evenly among 4 bowls and top with ricotta mixture.

Per serving (⅔ cup): 161 Cal, 4 g Total Fat, 2 g Sat Fat, 142 mg Sod, 22 g Total Carb, 5 g Sugar, 2 g Fib, 8 g Prot.

Add this
Our polenta-ricotta dish is truly satisfying as is, but you can sprinkle finely grated lemon or orange zest or ground cinnamon over it for another layer of flavor.

Red, white, and
blue parfaits

Red, white, and blue parfaits

Serves 4

2	**cups plain low-fat yogurt**
2	**tbsp chia seeds**
½	**tsp grated lemon zest**
2	**cups mixed berries (raspberries, blueberries, and sliced strawberries)**
½	**cup low-fat granola**

1 In a medium bowl, combine yogurt, chia seeds, and lemon zest. Cover and refrigerate until chia seeds have softened, at least 4 hours or overnight.

2 Into each of 4 mason jars or glasses, spoon ½ cup yogurt mixture. Top each with ½ cup berries and 2 tbsp granola.

Per serving (generous 1 cup): 186 Cal, 4 g Total Fat, 2 g Sat Fat, 118 mg Sod, 30 g Total Carb, 17 g Sugar, 5 g Fib, 9 g Prot.

Chapter 2
Opening act

Gin-basil smash, 27

Watermelon mojitos, 28

Mango-coconut agua fresca, 29

Coconut-cucumber splash, 31

Lotsa fruit spritzers, 32

Mustardy deviled eggs, 33

Chunky guacamole–topped rice cakes, 34

Crab salad–topped cucumber, 36

Greek tzatziki dip, 37

Provençal tomato tart, 38

Edamame-tomato bruschetta, 40

Reuben-style quesadillas, 41

Parmesan-pepper green bean "fries," 43

Root vegetable chips, 44

Cheesy kale crisps, 45

Lemon and pecorino popcorn, 47

Gin-basil
smash

Gin-basil smash

Serves 6

Muddle, don't mash! Using a muddler, which resembles a wooden pestle, or a wooden spoon, lightly crush the basil leaves, giving the muddler a few gentle twists as you go. When the basil aroma wafts into the air, you're done.

⅓ **cup lightly packed Thai, lemon, or regular basil leaves, plus more for garnish**

1 **cup gin**

½ **cup lemon juice**

3 **to 4 tbsp light agave nectar**

1 **cup ice cubes, plus more for serving**

1 Put basil into a cocktail shaker and gently muddle with muddler or wooden spoon.

2 Add all remaining ingredients; cover and shake vigorously until outside of shaker looks icy.

3 Strain gin mixture into 4 ice-filled wineglasses. Garnish with basil leaves.

Per serving (about ⅓ cup without ice): 96 Cal, 0 g Total Fat, 0 g Sat Fat, 1 mg Sod, 3 g Total Carb, 2 g Sugar, 0 g Fib, 0 g Prot.

Serving idea
Turn this drink into a spritzer by topping off each serving with seltzer.

Watermelon mojitos

Serves 6

The mojito, a world-famous Cuban cocktail, has been around since the early 20th century. While it's traditionally made with rum, we found that fresh watermelon pairs better with vodka, which is more lightly flavored.

⅓ **cup lightly packed mint leaves**

6 **cups tightly packed 1½-inch watermelon chunks**

1 **cup vodka**

¼ **cup lime juice**

1 **tbsp light agave nectar (or to taste)**

Ice cubes

Watermelon spears, thinly sliced lime, and/or fresh mint sprigs, for garnish

1 Put mint into a pitcher and gently muddle with muddler or wooden spoon.

2 Put watermelon into a blender and blend on low speed until smooth. Pour puree through a fine-mesh sieve set over a medium bowl, pressing hard on solids to extract all liquid; discard solids. Skim off foam from watermelon juice and discard.

3 To pitcher, add watermelon juice and stir in vodka, lime juice, and agave. Pour into 6 ice-filled glasses. Garnish with watermelon spears, lime slices, and/or mint sprigs.

Per serving (about 1 cup without ice): 147 Cal, 1 g Total Fat, 0 g Sat Fat, 4 mg Sod, 15 g Total Carb, 12 g Sugar, 1 g Fib, 1 g Prot.

Mango-coconut agua fresca

Serves 8

To cut and pit a mango, stand it on a long side; hold a sharp knife slightly off center; and carefully slice through the flesh, cutting off an oval "steak" of mango to separate it from the pit. Repeat on the other side.

4 **cups pure coconut water, preferably with pulp**

2 **ripe mangoes, peeled, pitted, and cubed (about 3 cups)**

3 **to 4 tbsp lime juice**

Ice-cold water

Ice cubes

Lime wedges, for garnish

1 In a blender, combine coconut water and mango and blend until smooth. Stir in lime juice and add enough ice-cold water to equal 8 cups.

2 Pour into 8 ice-filled glasses and garnish with lime wedges.

Per serving (1 cup without ice): 65 Cal, 0 g Total Fat, 0 g Sat Fat, 37 mg Sod, 17 g Total Carb, 14 g Sugar, 1 g Fib, 1 g Prot.

Coconut-
cucumber
splash

Coconut-cucumber splash

Serves 4

This is the perfect time to take advantage of spearmint growing in your garden or window-box container. Add a tangle of fragrant mint sprigs to this refresher for another layer of summertime flavor.

1 **(33½-oz) carton coconut water, chilled**

1 **mini cucumber, thinly sliced on diagonal**

Juice of 1 lime

1 **tbsp light agave nectar**

1 **tbsp grated peeled ginger or refrigerated ginger paste**

Ice cubes

1 Pour coconut water into large pitcher. Add cucumber, lime juice, agave, and ginger, stirring until mixed well.

2 Refrigerate at least 2 hours or up to 1 day. Pour into 4 ice-filled glasses.

Per serving (1 cup without ice): 63 Cal, 5 g Total Fat, 4 g Sat Fat, 66 mg Sod, 4 g Total Carb, 2 g Sugar, 1 g Fib, 0 g Prot.

Lotsa fruit spritzers

Serves 6

1½ cups well-chilled cran-strawberry juice

1½ cups well-chilled guava–passion fruit juice or tropical fruit medley

Juice of 1 large lime

3 cups well-chilled plain seltzer

Ice cubes

Lime wedges and whole strawberries, for garnish

Stir together cran-strawberry juice, guava–passion fruit juice, and lime juice in pitcher. Add seltzer and pour into 6 ice-filled glasses. Garnish with lime wedges and strawberries.

Per serving (1 cup without ice): 66 Cal, 0 g Total Fat, 0 g Sat Fat, 45 mg Sod, 17 g Total Carb, 14 g Sugar, 1 g Fib, 1 g Prot.

Mustardy deviled eggs

Serves 6

Our deviled eggs recipe rivals any version you've had of this American classic. A small amount of piquant Dijon mustard mixed with just a touch of white vinegar is what makes this rendition special.

6	**large eggs**
3	**tbsp reduced-fat mayonnaise**
1½	**tsp Dijon mustard**
1	**tsp white vinegar**
¼	**tsp hot pepper sauce**
¼	**tsp black pepper, plus more for sprinkling**
⅛	**tsp salt**

1 Put eggs in a medium saucepan and add enough cold water to cover by at least 1 inch; bring to a boil. Immediately remove saucepan from heat. Let stand, covered, 12 minutes. Pour off water and rinse eggs under cold running water to cool slightly.

2 Peel eggs and cut lengthwise in half. Remove yolks and transfer to a small bowl; mash with a fork until smooth. Add all remaining ingredients and stir until well combined.

3 Spoon yolk mixture into a small plastic bag and snip off one corner or spoon mixture into a pastry bag fitted with star tip. Evenly pipe mixture into egg-white halves. On a platter, arrange deviled eggs and sprinkle with black pepper. Serve or cover loosely and refrigerate up to 4 hours. Let stand 15 minutes at room temperature before serving for best flavor.

Per serving (2 deviled egg halves): 98 Cal, 7 g Total Fat, 2 g Sat Fat, 207 mg Sod, 1 g Total Carb, 1 g Sugar, 0 g Fib, 6 g Prot.

Chunky guacamole–topped rice cakes

Serves 4

If you're someone who likes finely diced red onion or chopped fresh cilantro in your guacamole, don't hesitate to add them to our tasty guac.

1	**Hass avocado, halved, pitted, and peeled**
1	**plum tomato, chopped**
½	**jalapeño pepper, seeded and minced**
2	**tsp lime juice**
¼	**tsp salt**
4	**(4-inch) thin square rice cakes, such as brown rice or rice-quinoa blend**

In a medium bowl, coarsely mash avocado. Add tomato, jalapeño, lime juice, and salt, gently stirring to combine. Top rice cakes evenly with guacamole and arrange on a platter.

Per serving (1 guacamole-topped rice cake): 123 Cal, 8 g Total Fat, 1 g Sat Fat, 152 mg Sod, 13 g Total Carb, 1 g Sugar, 4 g Fib, 2 g Prot.

Chunky guacamole-topped rice cakes

Crab salad-topped cucumber

Serves 4

The crab salad—simple and elegant—is delectable as is. But when a bit of flavor oomph is called for, add a generous squeeze of lime or lemon juice, as well as a pinch of cayenne or a few shakes of your favorite hot sauce.

¼　**lb lump crabmeat, picked over and flaked**

2　**tbsp mayonnaise**

2　**tbsp finely chopped chives**

1　**tbsp finely chopped celery**

¼　**tsp salt**

⅛　**tsp black pepper**

20　**(¼-inch) slices English (seedless) cucumber**

1 In a small bowl, gently stir together crabmeat, mayonnaise, chives, celery, salt, and pepper.

2 Onto each cucumber slice, spoon about 1 tsp crab mixture. Arrange on a platter and serve or loosely cover and refrigerate up to 2 hours.

Per serving (5 crab-topped cucumber slices): 78 Cal, 6 g Total Fat, 1 g Sat Fat, 276 mg Sod, 1 g Total Carb, 1 g Sugar, 0 g Fib, 6 g Prot.

Greek tzatziki dip

Serves 6

Who doesn't love tzatziki, the Greek cucumber-yogurt dip? Nothing could be easier than a recipe where stirring ingredients together in a bowl is all that's required.

½ **English (seedless) cucumber, cut into ¼-inch dice**

1 **cup plain reduced-fat Greek yogurt**

2 **tbsp chopped dill**

1 **tsp ground cumin**

¼ **tsp salt**

⅛ **to ¼ tsp black pepper**

In a serving bowl, stir together all ingredients. Serve immediately or cover and refrigerate up to 4 days.

Per serving (scant ⅓ cup): 32 Cal, 1 g Total Fat, 1 g Sat Fat, 112 mg Sod, 3 g Total Carb, 1 g Sugar, 0 g Fib, 4 g Prot.

Try this
If you've never added diced ripe mango to tzatziki, this is your opportunity. It adds a welcome bit of fruitiness to this dip.

Provençal tomato tart

Serves 12

In this tasty pick-up-and-eat appetizer, a light and crisp phyllo-dough shell surrounds juicy slices of ripe tomato. Scattered on top are temptingly salty Kalamata olives and grated Parmesan, while ever-so-thinly-sliced onion adds the right touch.

Olive-oil nonstick spray

5 large red or yellow plum tomatoes or a combination, cut into ¼-inch slices

1 onion, very thinly sliced

16 pitted Kalamata olives, quartered

½ tsp salt

¼ tsp black pepper

8 (12 x 17-inch) sheets phyllo dough, thawed if frozen

½ cup grated Parmesan

1 Set oven rack in lower third of oven and preheat oven to 425°F.

2 Meanwhile, between double layers of paper towels, place tomato slices and pat dry. Let stand 10 minutes.

3 In a small bowl, toss together onion, olives, salt, and pepper.

4 On a large baking sheet, lay 1 phyllo-dough sheet and lightly spray with nonstick spray. (Keep remaining phyllo covered with a damp kitchen towel and plastic wrap to prevent it from drying out.) Repeat layering with remaining 7 sheets of phyllo, spraying each sheet with nonstick spray. Roll in edges of phyllo to form a rim.

5 In a single overlapping layer, arrange tomato slices on phyllo dough. Top with onion mixture and lightly spray with nonstick spray. Bake until bottom and edges of phyllo dough are golden and tomatoes and onion are softened, 25 to 35 minutes. Sprinkle with Parmesan. Cut tart into 12 equal pieces. Serve hot, warm, or at room temperature.

Per serving (1 piece): 72 Cal, 3 g Total Fat, 1 g Sat Fat, 273 mg Sod, 10 g Total Carb, 1 g Sugar, 1 g Fib, 3 g Prot.

**Provençal
tomato tart**

Edamame-tomato bruschetta

Serves 6

¾ **lb tomatoes,**
  cut into small dice

¾ **tsp salt, divided**

½ **tsp black pepper, divided**

1½ **cups frozen shelled**
  edamame

2 **tbsp extra-virgin**
  olive oil, divided

12 **(½-inch) slices whole-**
  wheat or whole-grain
  Italian bread, toasted

1 **lemon, cut into 6 wedges**

1 In a large bowl, stir together tomatoes, ¼ tsp salt, and ¼ tsp pepper. Let stand until tomato juices are released, about 20 minutes. In a sieve set over small bowl, drain tomato mixture; reserve juice.

2 Cook edamame according to package directions. Drain and let cool.

3 In a food processor, combine edamame, ⅓ cup reserved tomato juice, 1 tbsp oil, remaining ½ tsp salt, and remaining ¼ tsp pepper until it forms a coarse puree, adding a little tomato juice or water if mixture seems dry.

4 Spread 1 rounded tbsp edamame puree on each toast and top evenly with tomatoes. Drizzle remaining 1 tbsp oil over tomatoes and serve with lemon wedges.

Per serving (2 bruschetta): 273 Cal, 9 g Total Fat, 1 g Sat Fat, 588 mg Sod, 35 g Total Carb, 6 g Sugar, 6 g Fib, 13 g Prot.

Add this
Sprinkle each bruschetta with thinly sliced mint or basil for a touch of bright flavor.

Reuben-style quesadillas

Serves 8

A Reuben is a classic deli sandwich of corned beef, coleslaw, Swiss cheese, Thousand Island dressing, and sauerkraut layered between slices of bread. We've slimmed it down by substituting roast turkey for the corned beef.

Nonstick spray

½ **cup Thousand Island dressing**

4 **(7-inch) reduced-fat whole-wheat tortillas**

1 **(¼-lb) piece skinless roasted turkey, shredded**

1 **cup tightly packed coleslaw mix**

½ **cup shredded reduced-fat Swiss cheese**

1 Spread 1 tbsp dressing on ½ of each tortilla. Layer ¼ turkey, coleslaw, and Swiss cheese over dressing. Fold unfilled half of each tortilla over filling, gently pressing down. Spray tops of quesadillas with nonstick spray.

2 In a large skillet over medium-high heat, place 2 quesadillas, sprayed-side down. Cook until crisp and browned in spots, about 3 minutes. Spray tops of quesadillas with nonstick spray and turn over. Cook until browned in spots and cheese is melted, about 2 minutes longer.

3 Transfer quesadillas to cutting board and cover to keep warm. Repeat with remaining 2 quesadillas. Cut each quesadilla in half. Serve with remaining ¼ cup dressing.

Per serving (½ quesadilla and 1½ tsp dressing): 154 Cal, 7 g Total Fat, 1 g Sat Fat, 314 mg Sod, 15 g Total Carb, 4 g Sugar, 1 g Fib, 8 g Prot.

Serving idea
We left the sauerkraut out of our Reuben quesadillas. If you'd like, however, spread a thin layer of well-drained canned or bagged sauerkraut over the slaw.

**Parmesan-pepper
green bean "fries"**

Parmesan-pepper green bean "fries"

Serves 6

2 **large egg whites,
   at room temperature**

2 **tbsp water**

1 **cup grated Parmesan**

1 **tsp black pepper**

¾ **lb green beans,
   trimmed**

1 Preheat oven to 425°F. Line a large rimmed baking sheet with silicone baking mat or sheet of parchment paper.

2 In a shallow bowl, whisk together egg whites and water until foamy. In another shallow bowl, mix together Parmesan and pepper.

3 Dip green beans, one at a time, into egg-white mixture, allowing excess to drip off. Coat beans with Parmesan and arrange on prepared baking sheet, about 1 inch apart.

4 Bake until Parmesan is melted and lightly browned, about 8 minutes. Transfer green beans on baking sheet to wire rack and let cool slightly before serving.

Per serving (⅙ of green beans): 94 Cal, 5 g Total Fat, 3 g Sat Fat, 323 mg Sod, 7 g Total Carb, 1 g Sugar, 2 g Fib, 7 g Prot.

Root vegetable chips

Serves 8

Crisp vegetable chips have taken off as a smarter-than-potato-chips snack choice—and for good reason. They have better stats and are über flavorful. Ours are no exception.

Olive-oil nonstick spray

1   very large carrot, peeled

1   very large parsnip, peeled

1   small sweet potato, scrubbed

¾   tsp kosher salt

Pinch cayenne

1 Preheat oven to 400°F. Line two large rimmed baking sheets with nonstick foil.

2 Cut carrot, parsnip, and sweet potato into ⅛-inch slices using a vegetable slicer or the thin slicing blade of food processor. In a large bowl, combine vegetables and generously spray with nonstick spray, tossing to coat evenly. Sprinkle vegetables with salt and cayenne, tossing to coat.

3 On prepared baking sheets, arrange vegetables in single layer. Bake until lightly browned, about 30 minutes, rotating sheets halfway through baking time and transferring vegetables to a large bowl as they are browned. (Chips will crisp a bit as they cool.)

Per serving (about ½ cup): 41 Cal, 0 g Total Fat, 0 g Sat Fat, 199 mg Sod, 10 g Total Carb, 3 g Sugar, 2 g Fib, 1 g Prot.

Cheesy kale crisps

Serves 8

Kale chips, also known as crisps, have become all the rage. Making them at home is easy and much less expensive than buying them. Store the chips in an airtight container up to several days.

Nonstick spray

2 **bunches curly kale, tough stems removed and discarded and leaves torn into 2-inch pieces**

4 **tsp canola oil**

1 **tsp garlic powder**

½ **tsp onion powder**

½ **tsp kosher salt**

3 **tbsp grated Pecorino Romano**

1 Preheat oven to 350°F. Spray two large baking sheets with nonstick spray.

2 Put kale in very large bowl. Drizzle with oil and toss until evenly coated. Sprinkle with garlic powder, onion powder, and salt and toss until mixed well.

3 Spread kale on prepared baking sheets to form single layer. Bake until crisp, about 20 minutes. Let cool slightly; sprinkle with Pecorino Romano.

Per serving (about 1¼ cups): 74 Cal, 4 g Total Fat, 1 g Sat Fat, 187 mg Sod, 8 g Total Carb, 2 g Sugar, 3 g Fib, 4 g Prot.

Lemon and pecorino popcorn

Lemon and pecorino popcorn

Serves 8

It might surprise you to know that the oldest popped kernels of corn were discovered in a cave in New Mexico back in 1948. The popped corn was then carbon-dated and shown to be about 5,600 years old!

8	cups plain air-popped popcorn
1	tbsp olive oil
1	tbsp chopped thyme
1	tsp grated lemon zest
½	tsp salt
6	tbsp grated Pecorino Romano

Put popcorn into a very large bowl. Drizzle with oil, thyme, lemon zest, and salt, tossing to coat popcorn evenly. Gradually sprinkle Pecorino Romano over popcorn, tossing to coat evenly.

Per serving (1 cup): 61 Cal, 3 g Total Fat, 1 g Sat Fat, 222 mg Sod, 6 g Total Carb, 0 g Sugar, 1 g Fib, 2 g Prot.

Chapter 3
Big and small soups and salads

Silky chickpea soup with cumin, 50

Fresh corn-basil soup, 52

Miso soup with tofu and scallions, 53

North African red lentil soup, 54

Soba noodle–mushroom soup, 57

Pea soup with smoked salmon, 59

Simple potato-leek soup, 60

Thai egg drop soup, 61

Coconut-curry tomato soup, 62

Chickpea-broccoli soup, 63

Roast beef and Napa cabbage slaw, 64

Greens with Gorgonzola and almonds, 65

Niçoise-inspired tuna salad, 67

Warm roasted butternut squash salad, 68

Romaine and sun-dried tomato salad, 70

South-of-the-border salad, 71

Chunky cucumber-yogurt salad, 72

Fresh pea salad with bacon, 74

Double orange–mint salad, 75

Red quinoa salad with oranges, 76

Sumac-dusted onion and chickpeas, 78

Silky chickpea soup with cumin

Serves 6

Chickpea (garbanzo) flour is made from ground dried chickpeas. It can be found in most supermarkets—look for Bob's Red Mill—and in specialty-food stores. It's used to make socca, crêpes that are sold on the streets of Provence.

1	**tbsp cumin seeds**
5½	**cups water, divided**
2	**large garlic cloves, minced**
1¼	**tsp salt**
1	**cup chickpea flour**
2	**tbsp lemon juice, plus 6 very thin lemon wedges**
1	**tbsp fruity extra-virgin olive oil**

1 Put cumin seeds in a medium saucepan and toast over medium heat, shaking pan occasionally, until seeds deepen slightly in color and are fragrant, about 2 minutes. Transfer ½ tsp toasted seeds to cup and reserve.

2 To the same saucepan, add 4½ cups water, garlic, and salt and bring to a boil. Reduce heat and simmer until flavors are blended, about 5 minutes.

3 Meanwhile, in a medium bowl or glass measure, whisk together chickpea flour and remaining 1 cup water, then gradually whisk into water-garlic mixture in saucepan. Cook, whisking occasionally, until soup has thickened, about 3 minutes.

4 Remove saucepan from heat and stir in lemon juice. Ladle soup evenly into 6 bowls and sprinkle with reserved cumin seeds. Drizzle each serving with ½ tsp oil and top with a lemon slice.

Per serving (1 cup): 88 Cal, 4 g Total Fat, 0 g Sat Fat, 503 mg Sod, 11 g Total Carb, 2 g Sugar, 2 g Fib, 4 g Prot.

**Silky chickpea soup
with cumin**

Fresh corn-basil soup

Serves 6

1	tbsp canola oil
1	onion, chopped
3	large garlic cloves, minced
3	cups corn kernels (about 6 ears of corn)
1	(32-oz) carton vegetable broth
½	tsp salt
¼	tsp black pepper
	Thinly sliced basil leaves

1 In a large pot or Dutch oven over medium heat, warm oil. Add onion and cook, stirring, until softened, about 5 minutes. Add garlic and cook, stirring, until fragrant, about 30 seconds. Add corn and cook, stirring, until tender, about 5 minutes. Stir in broth, salt, and pepper and bring to boil. Reduce heat and simmer 10 minutes. Remove pot from heat and let cool 10 minutes.

2 Transfer 3 cups of soup to blender and blend until smooth. Return to pot and cook over low heat until heated through, about 2 minutes. Ladle soup evenly into 6 bowls and sprinkle with basil.

Per serving (1 cup): 137 Cal, 4 g Total Fat, 0 g Sat Fat, 649 mg Sod, 26 g Total Carb, 6 g Sugar, 3 g Fib, 4 g Prot.

Miso soup with tofu and scallions

Serves 4

Lunch or dinner in a Japanese restaurant invariably begins with a choice of a green salad topped with carrot-ginger dressing or a bowl of delicately flavored miso soup studded with bits of scallion. Our flavorful rendition rivals any you've had.

4	**cups water**
1	**(14-oz) package firm tofu, diced**
½	**lb shiitake mushrooms, stems removed and caps thinly sliced**
6	**scallions, sliced (white and green parts separated)**
½	**tsp grated peeled ginger or refrigerated ginger paste, divided**
¼	**cup white miso**
¼	**tsp black pepper**

1 In a medium saucepan, bring water to a boil. Add tofu, mushrooms, white parts of scallions, and ¼ tsp ginger and bring to a boil again. Reduce heat and simmer until flavors are blended, about 5 minutes.

2 Ladle about ½ cup liquid into a small bowl and whisk in miso until smooth. Stir miso mixture back into saucepan and remove from heat.

3 Stir green part of scallions, remaining ¼ tsp ginger, and pepper into soup. Ladle soup evenly into 4 bowls.

Per serving (1¼ cups): 137 Cal, 5 g Total Fat, 1 g Sat Fat, 652 mg Sod, 13 g Total Carb, 2 g Sugar, 4 g Fib, 13 g Prot.

North African red lentil soup

Serves 4

Simple yet exotic is the best way to describe this boldly flavored soup. The marriage of tomatoes with red lentils, ground cumin, cilantro, and yogurt will transport you to far-flung places where you've always dreamed of traveling.

3	**cups water**
1	**(14½-oz) can diced tomatoes with garlic and onions**
1	**cup dried red lentils, picked over and rinsed**
1	**tsp ground cumin**
¾	**tsp salt**
¼	**tsp black pepper**
⅓	**cup chopped cilantro**
½	**cup plain low-fat yogurt**

1 In a medium saucepan, combine water, tomatoes, lentils, cumin, salt, and pepper. Bring to a boil. Reduce heat and simmer, covered, stirring occasionally, until lentils are tender, about 30 minutes.

2 Remove saucepan from heat and stir in cilantro. Ladle soup evenly into 4 bowls. Top each serving with 2-tbsp dollop yogurt. If reheating, thin soup with water as needed.

Per serving (1 cup soup and 2 tbsp yogurt): 218 Cal, 1 g Total Fat, 0 g Sat Fat, 861 mg Sod, 38 g Total Carb, 7 g Sugar, 6 g Fib, 14 g Prot.

**North African
red lentil soup**

Soba noodle–mushroom soup

Soba noodle–mushroom soup

Serves 6

3 oz soba (100% buckwheat) noodles

6 cups chicken broth

1 tbsp white miso

¼ lb shiitake mushrooms, stems removed and caps sliced

4 cups lightly packed baby spinach

1 Cook noodles according to package directions. Drain in a colander and rinse under cool running water; drain again.

2 Meanwhile, in a large saucepan, whisk together broth and miso. Add mushrooms and bring to boil. Reduce heat and simmer until mushrooms are tender, about 5 minutes. Stir in noodles and spinach and cook until noodles are heated through and spinach has wilted, about 3 minutes longer.

Per serving (about 1 cup): 105 Cal, 2 g Total Fat, 0 g Sat Fat, 883 mg Sod, 14 g Total Carb, 2 g Sugar, 2 g Fib, 8 g Prot.

Serving idea
To make this soup heartier, add ¼ lb cooked small shrimp (pictured) or picked over lump crabmeat along with the noodles in step 2. Dress up each serving by sprinkling with chopped chives, if you'd like.

**Pea soup with
smoked salmon**

Pea soup with smoked salmon

Serves 6

Smoked salmon and chives are a wonderful match. Sprinkle each serving of soup with finely chopped fresh chives for a bit of delicate onion flavor.

2	**(14½-oz) cans chicken broth**
1	**large baking potato, peeled and diced**
1	**onion, chopped**
1	**(16-oz) bag frozen baby peas**
¼	**tsp salt**
¼	**plus ⅛ tsp black pepper, divided**
2	**oz thinly sliced smoked salmon, diced or cut crosswise into thin strips**

1 In a large saucepan, combine broth, potato, and onion and bring to a boil. Reduce heat and simmer until potato is fork-tender, about 10 minutes. Stir in peas, salt, and ¼ tsp pepper and cook until peas are tender, about 5 minutes.

2 Remove saucepan from heat and let cool 10 minutes. Pour soup into a blender, in batches if needed, and blend until smooth. Return soup to saucepan and cook over low heat until heated through, about 2 minutes. Ladle soup evenly into 6 bowls, top with salmon, and sprinkle with remaining ⅛ tsp pepper.

Per serving (1 cup soup and 1½ tbsp smoked salmon): 145 Cal, 2 g Total Fat, 0 g Sat Fat, 788 mg Sod, 23 g Total Carb, 6 g Sugar, 5 g Fib, 10 g Prot.

Simple potato-leek soup

Serves 6

To clean leeks, trim the roots, leaving the root ends intact. Cut the leeks lengthwise in half and fan open the layers. Swish the leeks in a large bowl of cool water to release any grit. Lift out the leeks and slice or chop as directed.

1¾	**lb Yukon Gold potatoes, peeled and cut into ¾-inch chunks**
4	**large leeks (white and pale green parts only), thinly sliced**
1	**large onion, chopped**
5	**cups chicken broth**
½	**tsp salt**
¼	**tsp black pepper**
	Chopped chives

1 In a large pot or Dutch oven, combine potatoes, leeks, onion, broth, salt, and pepper. Bring to a boil. Reduce heat and simmer, covered, until vegetables are tender, about 25 minutes. Remove pot from heat and let cool 10 minutes.

2 Pour soup into a blender, in batches if needed, and blend until smooth. Return soup to pot and cook over low heat until heated through, about 2 minutes. Taste and season with salt and pepper, if needed. Ladle soup evenly into 6 bowls and sprinkle with chives.

Per serving (1⅓ cups): 175 Cal, 2 g Total Fat, 0 g Sat Fat, 849 mg Sod, 33 g Total Carb, 6 g Sugar, 5 g Fib, 8 g Prot.

Thai egg drop soup

Serves 4

We love this simple egg drop soup just the way it is, but you can also stir in a handful or two of tender watercress sprigs.

1	**(32-oz) carton chicken broth**
1	**tsp Thai green curry paste (or to taste)**
3	**large eggs, lightly beaten**
1	**small scallion, thinly sliced**
2	**tbsp chopped cilantro**
¼	**tsp salt (or to taste)**

1 In a large saucepan, whisk together broth and curry paste and bring to a boil. Reduce heat and simmer 8 minutes.

2 Gradually add eggs in slow, steady stream, gently stirring constantly to form threads of egg. Cook, stirring constantly, 1 minute. Remove saucepan from heat and stir in scallion, cilantro, and salt. Ladle evenly into 4 bowls.

Per serving (1 cup): 94 Cal, 5 g Total Fat, 2 g Sat Fat, 906 mg Sod, 2 g Total Carb, 1 g Sugar, 0 g Fib, 9 g Prot.

Coconut-curry tomato soup

Serves 4

This zesty soup will transport you to exotic places you've dreamed of traveling to. Cooking the curry paste in oil releases all its complexity. Coconut milk then rounds out the flavors, while tomatoes and lime juice add just the right note of acidity.

2	**tsp canola oil**
1¼	**tsp Thai red curry paste (or to taste)**
2	**(14½-oz) cans petite diced tomatoes**
1	**(13.66-oz) can light (low-fat) coconut milk**
¼	**tsp salt**
2	**tsp lime juice**
⅓	**cup lightly packed cilantro leaves, coarsely chopped**

1 In a large saucepan over medium heat, warm oil. Add curry paste and cook, stirring constantly, until fragrant, about 1 minute. Stir in tomatoes, coconut milk, and salt and bring to a boil. Reduce heat and simmer, covered, 3 minutes.

2 Remove saucepan from heat and stir in lime juice. Ladle soup evenly into 4 bowls and sprinkle with cilantro.

Per serving (1¼ cups): 130 Cal, 9 g Total Fat, 6 g Sat Fat, 462 mg Sod, 12 g Total Carb, 5 g Sugar, 2 g Fib, 2 g Prot.

Chickpea-broccoli soup

Serves 4

For a delicious variation on this fast and tasty soup, use cauliflower instead of the broccoli, and cannellini (white kidney) beans instead of the chickpeas.

2	tsp olive oil
1	large garlic clove, minced
2	cups water
1	cup canned crushed tomatoes
¼	tsp salt (or to taste)
¼	tsp black pepper (or to taste)
2	cups small broccoli florets
1	cup canned chickpeas, rinsed and drained
¼	cup grated Parmesan

1 In a medium saucepan over medium heat, warm oil. Add garlic and cook, stirring constantly, until fragrant, about 30 seconds.

2 Add water, tomatoes, salt, and pepper and bring to a boil. Add broccoli and chickpeas; reduce heat and simmer, covered, stirring occasionally, until broccoli is tender, about 5 minutes.

3 Ladle soup evenly into 4 bowls and sprinkle with Parmesan.

Per serving (about 1 cup soup and 1 tbsp Parmesan): 156 Cal, 6 g Total Fat, 1 g Sat Fat, 513 mg Sod, 20 g Total Carb, 5 g Sugar, 5 g Fib, 8 g Prot.

Try this
Before adding the garlic to the saucepan, cook 1 small onion, chopped, in the oil until softened, about 5 minutes, for another tasty layer of flavor.

Roast beef and Napa cabbage slaw

Serves 4

½ cup gluten-free reduced-fat sesame-ginger dressing, divided

2 tsp grated peeled ginger

6 cups lightly packed thinly sliced Napa cabbage

2 cups matchstick-cut carrots

6 (1-oz) slices lean roast beef, trimmed and cut into strips

Black pepper

In a large bowl, whisk together 6 tbsp dressing and ginger. Add cabbage and carrots and toss until coated evenly. Divide evenly among 4 plates and top evenly with roast beef. Sprinkle salads with pepper and drizzle with remaining 2 tbsp dressing.

Per serving (about 2 cups slaw and 1½ slices roast beef): 196 Cal, 6 g Total Fat, 1 g Sat Fat, 410 mg Sod, 23 g Total Carb, 14 g Sugar, 5 g Fib, 14 g Prot.

Greens with Gorgonzola and almonds

Serves 4

5 tbsp reduced-fat raspberry vinaigrette

1 shallot, thinly sliced

1 (7-oz) container mixed baby salad greens

¼ cup crumbled Gorgonzola or goat cheese

2 tbsp chopped smoked almonds

In a large bowl, combine vinaigrette and shallot. Add salad greens and toss until coated evenly. Add Gorgonzola and toss until combined. Divide salad evenly among 4 plates and sprinkle with almonds.

Per serving (1½ cups salad and ½ tbsp almonds): 129 Cal, 10 g Total Fat, 3 g Sat Fat, 509 mg Sod, 5 g Total Carb, 2 g Sugar, 2 g Fib, 6 g Prot.

**Niçoise-inspired
tuna salad**

Niçoise-inspired tuna salad

Serves 4

Niçoise salad originated in the city of Nice in France. Serve our version on a bed of Bibb lettuce leaves.

Grated zest and juice of 1 large lemon

2   cups packaged fully cooked diced potatoes, at room temperature

1   large tomato, diced

16   Niçoise olives, pitted if desired

½   tsp salt

¼   tsp black pepper

1   (5-oz) can water-packed light tuna, drained and flaked

In a serving bowl, combine lemon zest and juice. Add potatoes, tomato, olives, salt, and pepper and toss until mixed well. Gently stir in tuna.

Per serving (about 1 cup): 138 Cal, 2 g Total Fat, 0 g Sat Fat, 514 mg Sod, 22 g Total Carb, 2 g Sugar, 4 g Fib, 11 g Prot.

Warm roasted butternut squash salad

Serves 4

Olive-oil nonstick spray

1 (20-oz) package peeled and seeded butternut squash chunks

½ tsp salt

¼ tsp black pepper

1 (5-oz) container baby kale, baby arugula, mizuna, and radicchio salad mix

⅓ cup reduced-fat red-wine vinaigrette

¼ cup coarsely chopped walnuts, toasted

¼ cup crumbled soft goat cheese

1 Preheat oven to 425°F. Spray a rimmed baking sheet with nonstick spray.

2 Put squash on prepared baking sheet. Spray with nonstick spray and sprinkle with salt and pepper; toss until evenly coated and spread to form even layer.

3 Roast squash, turning halfway through roasting time, until tender and lightly browned, about 25 minutes. Let cool slightly.

4 Put salad mix in a large bowl. Drizzle with vinaigrette and toss until coated evenly. Divide salad evenly among 4 plates. Top evenly with squash and sprinkle with walnuts and goat cheese.

Per serving (2 cups greens, ¾ cup squash, 1 tbsp walnuts, and 1 tbsp goat cheese): 187 Cal, 10 g Total Fat, 3 g Sat Fat, 587 mg Sod, 21 g Total Carb, 5 g Sugar, 4 g Fib, 6 g Prot.

**Warm roasted
butternut squash salad**

Romaine and sun-dried tomato salad

Serves 4

Our red, white, and green salad mimics the colors of the boldly striped Italian flag. Save a bit of prep time by using moist-packed sun-dried tomatoes, which don't need to be soaked in hot water. You can find them in Italian markets and specialty-food stores.

16	**sun-dried tomato halves (not oil-packed)**
4	**cups lightly packed thinly sliced romaine lettuce**
4	**oz part-skim mozzarella, diced**
¼	**tsp salt**
¼	**tsp black pepper**
2	**tbsp good-quality balsamic vinegar**

1 In a small bowl, combine sun-dried tomatoes with enough hot water to cover and let stand until tomatoes have softened, about 10 minutes. Drain, pat dry with paper towels, and chop.

2 Meanwhile, in a salad bowl, combine romaine, mozzarella, salt, and pepper. Add sun-dried tomatoes and vinegar and toss until coated evenly.

Per serving (about 1⅓ cups): 108 Cal, 5 g Total Fat, 3 g Sat Fat, 335 mg Sod, 8 g Total Carb, 5 g Sugar, 2 g Fib, 9 g Prot.

Add this

For a welcome bit of crunch, sprinkle each serving of salad with ½ tbsp pumpkin seeds (pepitas).

South-of-the-border salad

Serves 6

1 poblano chile
4 cups lightly packed chopped romaine lettuce
2 cups matchstick-cut jicama (about ½ lb)
16 grape tomatoes, halved
½ cup black bean–corn salsa

1 Preheat broiler. Line a small heavy rimmed baking sheet with foil.

2 Place poblano on prepared baking sheet and broil 5 inches from heat, turning occasionally, until charred, about 5 minutes. Transfer chile to small zip-close plastic bag; seal and let steam about 10 minutes.

3 When cool enough to handle, remove charred peel and seeds from chile and discard. Coarsely chop chile and combine with romaine, jicama, tomatoes, and salsa in a salad bowl. Toss until mixed well.

Per serving (about 1 cup): 48 Cal, 1 g Total Fat, 0 g Sat Fat, 51 mg Sod, 11 g Total Carb, 3 g Sugar, 4 g Fib, 2 g Prot.

Chunky cucumber-yogurt salad

Serves 4

Because cucumbers tend to weep if they sit too long after being sliced, this salad is best eaten the day it's prepared.

¾ **cup plain low-fat yogurt**

2 **tsp white vinegar**

¼ **cup chopped dill**

½ **tsp salt**

¼ **tsp black pepper**

4 **cucumbers, peeled, halved lengthwise, seeded, and cut into ¼-inch slices**

1 **small red onion, very thinly sliced**

1 To make dressing: In a small bowl, whisk together yogurt, vinegar, dill, salt, and pepper.

2 Combine cucumbers and onion in a serving bowl. Add dressing and toss until coated evenly.

Per serving (1¼ cups): 64 Cal, 1 g Total Fat, 1 g Sat Fat, 328 mg Sod, 11 g Total Carb, 7 g Sugar, 2 g Fib, 4 g Prot.

Try this
Toss some chopped mint into the salad along with the yogurt and dill in step 1.

**Chunky cucumber-
yogurt salad**

Fresh pea salad with bacon

Serves 4

Mint and peas are a classic combo. If you happen to have fresh mint on hand—or growing in your garden—scatter thinly sliced or torn leaves over each serving.

1	**cup fresh or thawed frozen peas**
6	**slices packaged fully cooked bacon**
4	**oz pea shoots or sprouts**
2	**scallions, sliced**
⅓	**cup reduced-fat olive-oil vinaigrette**

1 Bring a small saucepan of water to a boil. Add peas and cook until tender, about 3 minutes. Drain in a colander and rinse under cold running water; drain again.

2 Heat bacon in microwave according to package directions. Crumble and set aside.

3 In a large bowl, combine peas, pea shoots, and scallions. Drizzle with vinaigrette and toss until coated evenly. Divide salad evenly among 4 plates and top with bacon.

Per serving (about 1½ cups salad and 1½ slices bacon): 125 Cal, 7 g Total Fat, 2 g Sat Fat, 550 mg Sod, 8 g Total Carb, 4 g Sugar, 3 g Fib, 7 g Prot.

Double orange–mint salad

Serves 6

This unusual salad, a great starter or side dish for grilled chicken breast or fish, gets its distinctive flavor from orange-flower water, which is distilled from orange blossoms and is used in Mediterranean cuisines.

3   **blood oranges, peeled, sliced into rounds, and seeded**

3   **navel oranges, peeled, sliced into rounds, and seeded**

¼   **to ½ tsp orange-flower water**

Pinch to ⅛ tsp finely ground black pepper

2   **tbsp confectioners' sugar**

24 **mint leaves, torn if large**

1 In a large bowl, combine oranges and sprinkle with orange-flower water; gently toss. Arrange oranges on a platter in a decorative pattern; sprinkle with pepper. Cover oranges with plastic wrap and refrigerate up to 1 hour.

2 To serve, dust oranges with confectioners' sugar and scatter mint leaves on top.

Per serving (1 orange): 85 Cal, 0 g Total Fat, 0 g Sat Fat, 0 mg Sod, 21 g Total Carb, 17 g Sugar, 4 g Fib, 2 g Prot.

Add this
Mix the confectioners' sugar with ¼ tsp ground cinnamon for an additional layer of flavor.

Red quinoa salad with oranges

Serves 4

A tangle of tempting textures and flavors best describes this unusual salad. Whole-grain, gluten-free quinoa is the perfect foil for the slightly bitter radishes, juicy navel oranges, and salty feta. If you've never had radish tops, this is your chance—you'll love 'em.

1	cup red quinoa, rinsed
3	navel oranges
4	large radishes with tops, radishes halved and thinly sliced and tops torn
¼	cup reduced-fat red-wine vinaigrette
½	tsp salt
¼	tsp black pepper
¼	cup plus 2 tbsp crumbled reduced-fat feta

1 Prepare quinoa according to package directions. Let cool.

2 Meanwhile, halve and squeeze juice from 1 orange (you should have about ⅓ cup). Pour into a salad bowl. Cut sections from remaining 2 oranges and add to bowl.

3 Add cooled quinoa, radishes and tops, vinaigrette, salt, and pepper to orange mixture and gently toss until mixed well. Sprinkle with feta.

Per serving (about 1 cup): 250 Cal, 6 g Total Fat, 1 g Sat Fat, 591 mg Sod, 42 g Total Carb, 10 g Sugar, 6 g Fib, 9 g Prot.

Red quinoa salad
with oranges

Sumac-dusted onion and chickpeas

Serves 6

Ground sumac, made from the dried berries of a sumac bush that grows in the Middle East and in parts of Italy, is a beautiful dark red powder with a somewhat coarse texture and a tart lemony flavor.

1	small red onion, thinly sliced (about ¾ cup)
2	tsp ground sumac
¼	cup plus 2 tsp reduced-fat balsamic vinaigrette
2	(15½-oz) cans chickpeas, rinsed and drained
½	cup lightly packed torn mint
¼	tsp salt (or to taste)

1 Put onion in a small bowl; sprinkle with sumac and drizzle with 2 tsp vinaigrette. Toss with your hands, gently massaging sumac into onion. Let stand, tossing occasionally, until onion is wilted, about 30 minutes.

2 Stir together chickpeas, mint, remaining ¼ cup vinaigrette, and salt in a serving bowl and top with onions.

Per serving (⅔ cup): 151 Cal, 4 g Total Fat, 0 g Sat Fat, 750 mg Sod, 22 g Total Carb, 1 g Sugar, 7 g Fib, 7 g Prot.

Serving idea
The addition of fresh fruit would add a bit of zing to this made-for-fall salad. Add diced apple and let it get coated with the vinaigrette.

**Sumac-dusted onion
and chickpeas**

Chapter 4
Main event

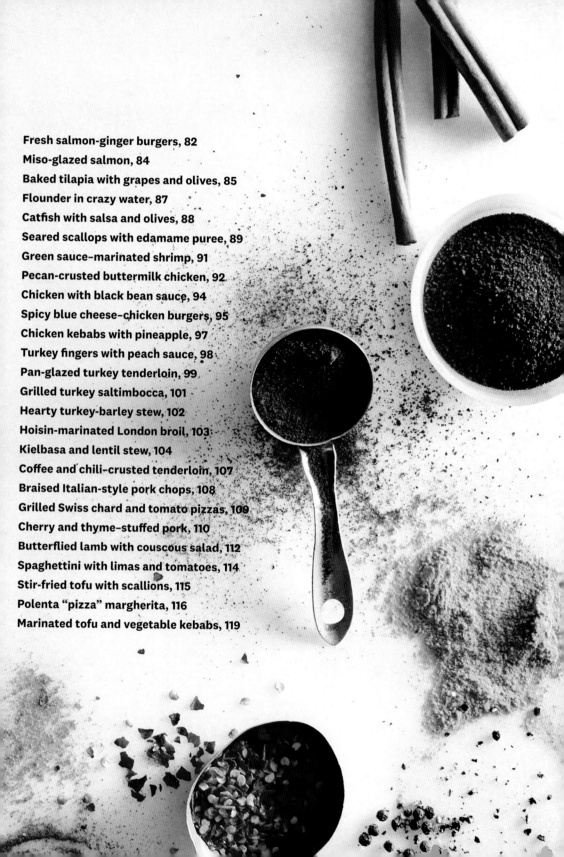

Fresh salmon-ginger burgers, 82

Miso-glazed salmon, 84

Baked tilapia with grapes and olives, 85

Flounder in crazy water, 87

Catfish with salsa and olives, 88

Seared scallops with edamame puree, 89

Green sauce–marinated shrimp, 91

Pecan-crusted buttermilk chicken, 92

Chicken with black bean sauce, 94

Spicy blue cheese–chicken burgers, 95

Chicken kebabs with pineapple, 97

Turkey fingers with peach sauce, 98

Pan-glazed turkey tenderloin, 99

Grilled turkey saltimbocca, 101

Hearty turkey-barley stew, 102

Hoisin-marinated London broil, 103

Kielbasa and lentil stew, 104

Coffee and chili–crusted tenderloin, 107

Braised Italian-style pork chops, 108

Grilled Swiss chard and tomato pizzas, 109

Cherry and thyme–stuffed pork, 110

Butterflied lamb with couscous salad, 112

Spaghettini with limas and tomatoes, 114

Stir-fried tofu with scallions, 115

Polenta "pizza" margherita, 116

Marinated tofu and vegetable kebabs, 119

Fresh salmon-ginger burgers

Serves 4

To get the most ginger flavor, shape the patties, place them on a wax paper–lined plate, and cover and refrigerate at least 2 hours or up to 6 hours before cooking so the flavor has time to develop.

1	slice white or whole-wheat sandwich bread
2	tbsp minced peeled ginger
8	tsp prepared horseradish sauce, such as cranberry-horseradish
1	lb skinless salmon fillet, cut into 1-inch pieces
¼	tsp salt
¼	tsp black pepper
2	tsp canola oil
¼	cup reduced-fat mayonnaise

1 Tear bread into pieces and pulse in a food processor until coarse crumbs form. Transfer crumbs to a large bowl and add ginger and 4 tsp of horseradish sauce. Put salmon into food processor and pulse until coarsely chopped. Add to crumb mixture along with salt and pepper.

2 With fork, gently stir salmon mixture until combined well but not overmixed. With damp hands, shape into 4 (4-inch) patties.

3 In a large nonstick skillet over medium heat, warm oil until hot. Add salmon patties and cook until golden brown and just opaque in center, about 3 minutes per side.

4 In a cup, stir together mayonnaise and remaining 4 tsp horseradish sauce. Dollop evenly onto salmon burgers.

Per serving (1 salmon burger and 1 tbsp sauce): 277 Cal, 18 g Total Fat, 4 g Sat Fat, 277 mg Sod, 5 g Total Carb, 1 g Sugar, 1 g Fib, 24 g Prot.

Try this

Get even more taste satisfaction by serving the burgers on whole-wheat sandwich thins with lettuce, tomato, and red onion.

Fresh salmon-ginger burgers

Miso-glazed salmon

Serves 4

2	**tbsp white miso**
2	**tbsp reduced-sodium soy sauce**
1½	**tsp honey**
4	**(5-oz) salmon fillets with skin**
4	**baby bok choy, halved lengthwise**

1 Line a small rimmed baking sheet with a sheet of nonstick foil.

2 Stir together miso, soy sauce, and honey in a cup. Put salmon on prepared baking sheet. Spoon miso mixture over salmon. Marinate in refrigerator at least 15 minutes or up to 2 hours, turning salmon once or twice.

3 Preheat oven to 425°F.

4 Bake salmon, skin-side down, until just opaque in center, about 15 minutes.

5 Meanwhile, place bok choy in a steamer basket set into a large skillet over 1 inch of boiling water. Cover and steam until bok choy is tender, about 6 minutes. To serve, slide spatula under salmon flesh to separate from skin. Serve salmon with bok choy.

Per serving (1 salmon fillet and 1 bok choy): 315 Cal, 8 g Total Fat, 1 g Sat Fat, 1,258 mg Sod, 23 g Total Carb, 14 g Sugar, 9 g Fib, 43 g Prot.

Baked tilapia with grapes and olives

Serves 4

Looking for a different fish to serve? Mild, white-fleshed, meaty tilapia is a great choice. It's always sold skinless and boneless and holds up well to pan-cooking, baking, grilling, and broiling. For the best choice, go to seafoodwatch.org.

Nonstick spray

1½ **cups seedless red grapes, halved**

½ **plus ⅛ tsp salt**

4 **(5-oz) tilapia fillets**

¼ **tsp black pepper**

⅓ **cup pitted Kalamata olives, chopped**

2 **tsp olive oil**

¼ **cup chopped flat-leaf parsley**

1 Preheat oven to 400°F. Spray a 9 x 13-inch baking dish with nonstick spray.

2 Spread grapes in prepared baking dish and sprinkle with ⅛ tsp salt. Bake 10 minutes.

3 Remove grapes from oven and stir. Sprinkle tilapia with pepper and remaining ½ tsp salt. Arrange fillets over grapes in single layer. Scatter olives on top of fish and drizzle with oil. Bake until fish is just opaque in center, about 15 minutes. Sprinkle with parsley.

Per serving (1 tilapia fillet and about ⅓ cup grapes): 205 Cal, 6 g Total Fat, 1 g Sat Fat, 560 mg Sod, 13 g Total Carb, 10 g Sugar, 1 g Fib, 27 g Prot.

Flounder in
crazy water

Flounder in crazy water

Serves 4

Pesce all'acqua pazza, which means "fish in crazy water," is a way of poaching fish that seems to have originated with Neapolitan fishermen who used sea water to cook their catch.

12	**large flat-leaf parsley sprigs**
2	**cups water**
4	**garlic cloves, thinly sliced**
4	**tsp extra-virgin olive oil**
¾	**tsp salt**
¾	**tsp black pepper**
1½	**lb mixed baby heirloom tomatoes (2 pints), halved or quartered if large**
4	**(5- to 6-oz) flounder fillets**

1 Separate leaves and stems of 8 parsley sprigs; coarsely chop leaves. Reserve remaining 4 sprigs. Place parsley stems in a large deep skillet with water, garlic, oil, salt, and pepper; bring to a boil. Reduce heat to medium-low and simmer, partially covered, until broth is fragrant and garlic is tender, about 15 minutes.

2 Remove parsley stems from skillet and discard. Add tomatoes and chopped parsley to skillet and return to a boil. Reduce heat and simmer, uncovered, until tomatoes are slightly softened, about 4 minutes. Fold ends of flounder under to form neat "packages." With a pancake spatula, place fish in skillet and cook, covered, until just opaque in center, about 7 minutes.

3 Using two spatulas, carefully transfer fillets to 4 large shallow bowls or deep plates. Spoon tomato mixture over fish and top with reserved 4 parsley sprigs.

Per serving (1 flounder fillet and generous ½ cup tomato mixture): 203 Cal, 7 g Total Fat, 1 g Sat Fat, 564 mg Sod, 8 g Total Carb, 4 g Sugar, 2 g Fib, 28 g Prot.

Catfish with salsa and olives

Serves 4

Green olives contribute an earthy, almost smoky, salty flavor to dishes. Brighten up a simple tomato sauce by adding a small amount of finely chopped olives for some depth of flavor or add chopped olives to a favorite salad for some interest.

2	**tbsp all-purpose flour**
¼	**tsp salt**
¼	**tsp black pepper**
4	**(6-oz) skinless catfish fillets**
1	**tbsp olive oil**
1⅓	**cups fat-free mild salsa**
¼	**cup pitted green olives, finely chopped**
2	**tbsp chopped flat-leaf parsley or cilantro**

1 Stir together flour, salt, and pepper on a sheet of wax paper. Coat catfish fillets, one at a time, with flour mixture, pressing so it adheres, shaking off any excess.

2 In a large heavy nonstick skillet over medium-high heat, warm oil. Add catfish, in batches if needed, and cook until golden, about 6 minutes per side. Add salsa and olives. Reduce heat and simmer, occasionally spooning salsa mixture over fish, until just opaque throughout, about 5 minutes longer. Sprinkle with parsley.

Per serving (1 catfish fillet and 3 tbsp salsa mixture): 236 Cal, 9 g Total Fat, 2 g Sat Fat, 649 mg Sod, 9 g Total Carb, 3 g Sugar, 2 g Fib, 29 g Prot.

Serving idea
Pair this boldly flavored fish dish with cooked brown rice, for sopping up the tasty sauce.

Seared scallops with edamame puree

Serves 4

Sea scallops are usually sold wet—packed in a solution that prevents them from drying out. If your market sells dry, day-boat, or diver scallops, these are the ones to reach for, as they contain no additives.

1¾	**cups frozen shelled edamame**
¾	**tsp salt, divided**
1	**cup water**
⅓	**cup fat-free half-and-half, warmed**
½	**tsp black pepper**
1	**lemon, halved**
16	**large sea scallops (about 1½ lb), patted dry**
1½	**tsp canola oil**

1 Bring a small saucepan of water to a boil over high heat. Add edamame and ¼ tsp salt and cook until edamame are tender, about 10 minutes. With a slotted spoon, remove ¼ cup edamame and reserve.

2 Transfer remaining 1½ cups edamame with 1 cup water to a blender. Add half-and-half, ¼ tsp salt, and ¼ tsp of pepper and blend until it forms a smooth, thick puree, adding a bit more water if needed. Return puree to saucepan and add juice from 1 lemon half, stirring to combine. Keep warm over very low heat.

3 Sprinkle scallops with remaining ¼ tsp salt. In a large heavy nonstick skillet over medium-high heat, warm oil until very hot. Add 8 scallops and sear until deep golden brown and barely translucent in center, about 2 minutes per side. Transfer scallops to a plate and loosely cover with sheet of foil. Cook remaining 8 scallops.

4 Spoon edamame puree evenly onto 4 plates and top each serving with 4 scallops. Sprinkle with reserved edamame and remaining ¼ tsp pepper. Cut remaining lemon half into 4 wedges and place alongside scallops.

Per serving (4 scallops, ½ cup puree, and 1 tbsp edamame): 249 Cal, 7 g Total Fat, 1 g Sat Fat, 1,120 mg Sod, 17 g Total Carb, 4 g Sugar, 3 g Fib, 29 g Prot.

Green sauce–
marinated shrimp

Green sauce-marinated shrimp

Serves 4

Did you know that you can press unpeeled trimmed garlic cloves through a garlic press? The force of the press pushes the garlic out of its skin and through the holes of the press.

Nonstick spray

⅓   **cup chopped
     flat-leaf parsley**

⅓   **cup chopped basil**

2   **garlic cloves, crushed
     through a press**

4   **tsp olive oil**

¼   **tsp salt**

¼   **tsp black pepper**

1½ **lb large shrimp,
     peeled and deveined**

Lemon wedges

1 To make marinade, combine parsley, basil, garlic, oil, salt, and pepper in a large zip-close plastic bag; add shrimp. Squeeze out air and seal bag; turn to coat shrimp. Refrigerate, turning bag occasionally, at least 1 hour or up to 6 hours. Remove shrimp from marinade; discard marinade.

2 Spray a heavy nonstick ridged grill pan with nonstick spray and set over medium-high heat. Add shrimp, in batches if needed, and cook until just opaque in center, about 2 minutes per side. Serve with lemon wedges.

Per serving (about 9 shrimp): 168 Cal, 6 g Total Fat, 1 g Sat Fat, 1,112 mg Sod, 4 g Total Carb, 0 g Sugar, 1 g Fib, 24 g Prot.

Pecan-crusted buttermilk chicken

Serves 4

This chicken has it all! It's got a crunchy coating of finely chopped pecans and bread crumbs and a moist and tender interior, thanks to a good soak in low-fat buttermilk. For the best results, be sure to use a well-seasoned cast-iron skillet.

Nonstick spray

4   (5-oz) skinless
    boneless chicken breasts

¾   cup low-fat buttermilk

⅓   cup plain dried bread
    crumbs

¼   cup pecans, finely chopped

1   tsp Cajun seasoning

1   tbsp canola oil

1 In a medium bowl, combine chicken and buttermilk and turn until coated evenly. Refrigerate 20 minutes.

2 Meanwhile, preheat oven to 350°F.

3 Mix together bread crumbs, pecans, and Cajun seasoning on a sheet of wax paper. Remove 1 piece of chicken from buttermilk, allowing excess to drip off. Coat chicken with pecan mixture, gently pressing so it adheres. Place on separate sheet of wax paper. Repeat with remaining chicken. Lightly spray chicken on both sides with nonstick spray. Discard any remaining buttermilk and pecan mixture.

4 In a large heavy nonstick ovenproof skillet over medium-high heat, warm oil. Add chicken and cook until golden, about 2½ minutes per side. Transfer skillet to oven and bake until chicken is cooked through, about 10 minutes longer.

Per serving (1 chicken breast): 300 Cal, 13 g Total Fat, 2 g Sat Fat, 526 mg Sod, 10 g Total Carb, 3 g Sugar, 1 g Fib, 35 g Prot.

**Pecan-crusted
buttermilk chicken**

Chicken with black bean sauce

Serves 4

The key to success when it comes to cooking in a wok is allowing the wok to preheat enough so that the chicken starts to sear the minute it hits the pan. Just listen for the sizzle.

4	tsp dark sesame oil, divided
1	lb skinless boneless chicken breasts, cut on diagonal into strips
½	tsp salt
1	tbsp grated peeled ginger
1	(1-lb) bunch asparagus, trimmed and cut into 2-inch lengths
3	tbsp water
¼	cup black bean sauce

1 Heat a wok or large heavy deep nonstick skillet over medium-high heat until hot. Add 2 tsp oil, swirling to coat. Sprinkle chicken with salt and add to wok. Stir-fry until cooked through, about 3 minutes. Transfer to a plate.

2 Wipe out wok and heat remaining 2 tsp oil. Add ginger and stir-fry until fragrant, about 30 seconds. Add asparagus and water and cook, covered, until asparagus are crisp-tender, about 2 minutes.

3 Return chicken to wok along with black bean sauce. Stir-fry until chicken is heated through, about 1 minute longer.

Per serving (1¼ cups): 230 Cal, 9 g Total Fat, 2 g Sat Fat, 698 mg Sod, 7 g Total Carb, 3 g Sugar, 3 g Fib, 29 g Prot.

Spicy blue cheese–chicken burgers

Serves 4

Nonstick spray

1   **lb ground skinless chicken breast**

2   **scallions, thinly sliced**

3   **tbsp plain dried bread crumbs**

2   **tbsp hot pepper sauce, such as Frank's**

½   **tsp salt**

¼   **cup reduced-fat blue cheese dressing**

1 Mix together chicken, scallions, bread crumbs, pepper sauce, and salt in a medium bowl until combined well but not overmixed. With damp hands, shape mixture into 4 (4-inch) patties.

2 Spray a ridged grill pan with nonstick spray and set over medium heat. Spray patties with nonstick spray, place in pan and cook until instant-read thermometer inserted into side of burger registers 165°F, about 5 minutes per side. Drizzle burgers with blue cheese dressing.

Per serving (1 burger and 1 tbsp dressing): 200 Cal, 7 g Total Fat, 1 g Sat Fat, 706 mg Sod, 6 g Total Carb, 1 g Sugar, 0 g Fib, 27 g Prot.

**Chicken kebabs
with pineapple**

Chicken kebabs with pineapple

Serves 4

These kebabs were inspired by the Caribbean flavor combination of chicken, fresh pineapple, chile pepper, and lime. If you like heat, marinate the chicken overnight and, if you don't, 20 minutes will do the trick.

Nonstick spray

Grated zest and juice of 1 lime

1   **tbsp olive oil**

1   **jalapeño pepper, seeded and minced**

2   **garlic cloves, minced**

½   **tsp salt**

¼   **tsp black pepper**

1   **lb skinless boneless chicken breasts, cut into 1½-inch chunks**

1½   **cups pineapple chunks**

1   Combine lime juice, oil, jalapeño, garlic, salt, and black pepper in a large zip-close plastic bag; add chicken. Squeeze out air and seal bag; turn to coat chicken. Refrigerate, turning bag occasionally, at least 20 minutes or up to overnight.

2   Spray grill rack with nonstick spray. Preheat grill to medium or prepare medium fire. Soak 4 (8 to 10-inch) wooden skewers in water at least 20 minutes.

3   Remove chicken from marinade; discard marinade. Thread chicken and pineapple alternately onto skewers. Spray kebabs with nonstick spray and place on grill rack. Grill, turning occasionally, until chicken is cooked through, about 7 minutes. Sprinkle with lime zest.

Per serving (1 kebab): 209 Cal, 7 g Total Fat, 1 g Sat Fat, 343 mg Sod, 11 g Total Carb, 7 g Sugar, 1 g Fib, 26 g Prot.

Try this

Enjoy the kebabs along with some grilled bell peppers for more color and flavor.

Turkey fingers with peach sauce

Serves 4

To serve the turkey fingers as an appetizer, thread each cooked finger onto a small decorative wooden skewer for easy dipping.

Nonstick spray

½   **cup peach or apricot all-fruit spread**

1   **tsp curry powder**

1   **(1-lb) piece skinless boneless turkey breast**

¾   **tsp salt**

¼   **tsp black pepper**

½   **cup unsweetened flaked coconut, chopped**

¼   **cup whole-wheat panko bread crumbs**

1 Preheat oven to 425°F. Spray a rimmed baking sheet with nonstick spray.

2 To make sauce: In a bowl, stir together ¼ cup of all-fruit spread and ½ tsp of curry powder. Set aside.

3 Cut turkey into 16 strips. In a medium bowl, stir together remaining ¼ cup fruit spread, remaining ½ tsp curry powder, salt, and pepper. Add turkey and toss until coated evenly.

4 Mix together coconut and panko on a sheet of wax paper. Coat turkey strips, one at a time, in coconut mixture, lightly pressing so it adheres. Arrange turkey on prepared baking sheet in single layer and spray with nonstick spray. Bake until turkey fingers are golden and cooked through, about 15 minutes. Serve with reserved sauce.

Per serving (4 turkey fingers and 1 tbsp sauce): 305 Cal, 7 g Total Fat, 4 g Sat Fat, 592 mg Sod, 33 g Total Carb, 24 g Sugar, 2 g Fib, 28 g Prot.

Pan-glazed turkey tenderloin

Serves 4

Turkey tenderloin can sometimes be a bit more challenging to find in the meat case at a supermarket. So plan ahead and check with the butcher to see if it needs to be ordered.

⅓ **cup chicken broth**

¼ **cup apricot or peach all-fruit spread**

2 **tbsp Dijon mustard**

1½ **tsp chopped fresh thyme (or ½ tsp dried)**

1 **tbsp canola oil**

1 **(1-lb) piece skinless boneless turkey tenderloin**

½ **tsp salt**

¼ **tsp black pepper**

1 In a small bowl, stir together broth, fruit spread, mustard, and thyme.

2 In a large skillet over medium-high heat, warm oil. Sprinkle turkey with salt and pepper; add to skillet and cook, turning occasionally, until browned, about 5 minutes. Add apricot mixture and bring to a boil. Reduce heat and simmer, covered, until instant-read thermometer inserted into center of turkey registers 165°F, about 12 minutes longer.

3 Transfer turkey to a cutting board and let stand 5 minutes. Cut into 8 slices and serve with pan sauce.

Per serving (2 slices turkey and 2 tbsp sauce): 224 Cal, 5 g Total Fat, 1 g Sat Fat, 575 mg Sod, 15 g Total Carb, 10 g Sugar, 1 g Fib, 28 g Prot.

Serving idea

Turn the tenderloin into a complete meal by pairing it with a side of black beans sprinkled with diced red bell pepper and chopped cilantro.

Grilled turkey saltimbocca

Grilled turkey saltimbocca

Serves 4

Saltimbocca, which means "jumps in the mouth" in Italian, refers to the tasty combination of flavors in this Roman specialty. Soaking the wooden skewers in water ensures that they won't char on the grill.

Nonstick spray

32 **pencil (thin) asparagus spears (about ¾ lb), trimmed**

Ice water

4 **(¼-lb) turkey breast cutlets**

¼ **tsp salt**

¼ **tsp black pepper**

¼ **cup soft goat cheese**

12 **sage leaves**

8 **(½-oz) slices prosciutto**

1 Spray grill rack with nonstick spray. Preheat grill to medium or prepare medium fire. Soak 4 short wooden skewers in water at least 20 minutes.

2 Meanwhile, bring 1 inch of salted water to a boil in a large skillet. Add asparagus and cook, covered, until crisp-tender and bright green, about 2 minutes. With tongs, transfer to a bowl of ice water and let cool about 2 minutes. Drain asparagus on double layer of paper towels and pat dry.

3 Place turkey cutlets between two pieces of plastic wrap. With a meat mallet or rolling pin, lightly pound turkey to ¼-inch thickness. Remove top layer of plastic wrap and discard. Sprinkle turkey with salt and pepper. Spread 1 tbsp goat cheese on each cutlet. Place 8 asparagus spears crosswise on each cutlet and roll up beginning with short side. Place 3 sage leaves on each roll and wrap in 2 slices of prosciutto. Secure each roll with skewer and lightly spray with nonstick spray.

4 Place rolls on grill rack and grill, covered, turning occasionally, until turkey is cooked through, about 12 minutes. Remove skewers before eating.

Per serving (1 turkey roll): 303 Cal, 13 g Total Fat, 5 g Sat Fat, 1,154 mg Sod, 5 g Total Carb, 2 g Sugar, 3 g Fib, 43 g Prot.

Hearty turkey-barley stew

Serves 6

This stew is perfect for a chilly night in the fall or winter. If you happen to have fresh parsley on hand, toss in a small handful—coarsely chopped or torn—along with a couple of shakes of Worcestershire sauce just before serving.

1	**oz best-quality dried porcini mushrooms**
1½	**cups boiling water**
1	**tbsp olive oil**
1	**(1-lb) piece skinless boneless turkey tenderloin, cut into ½-inch pieces**
3	**leeks (white and pale green parts only), thinly sliced**
1	**(32-oz) carton chicken broth**
½	**cup pearl barley, rinsed**
¾	**tsp salt**
¼	**tsp black pepper**

1 In a small bowl, combine mushrooms and water and let soak until mushrooms have softened, about 10 minutes. Pour mushrooms and mushroom liquid through a paper towel–lined sieve set over a small bowl. Reserve mushroom liquid and coarsely chop mushrooms.

2 In a large saucepan over medium-high heat, warm oil. Add turkey and cook, stirring, until golden brown, about 8 minutes. Add leeks and cook, stirring, until softened, about 5 minutes. Add broth, barley, mushrooms and liquid, salt, and pepper and bring to boil. Reduce heat and simmer, covered, until barley is tender, about 30 minutes longer.

Per serving (1¼ cups): 231 Cal, 5 g Total Fat, 1 g Sat Fat, 846 mg Sod, 23 g Total Carb, 2 g Sugar, 4 g Fib, 24 g Prot.

Hoisin-marinated London broil

Serves 4

Hoisin sauce is a key ingredient in many Chinese dishes. This thick, dark, rich sauce is made from soy beans, fennel seeds, chiles, garlic, and vinegar.

Nonstick spray

¼	**cup hoisin sauce**
2	**large garlic cloves, minced**
1	**tbsp grated peeled ginger or refrigerated ginger paste**
1	**tbsp rice vinegar**
1	**(1-lb) lean boneless sirloin steak, trimmed**
½	**tsp salt**
¼	**tsp black pepper**

1 Combine hoisin sauce, garlic, ginger, and vinegar in a large zip-close plastic bag; add steak. Squeeze out air and seal bag; turn to coat steak. Refrigerate, turning bag occasionally, at least 4 hours or up to overnight.

2 Spray broiler rack with nonstick spray and preheat broiler.

3 Remove steak from marinade; discard marinade. Pat steak dry with paper towels and sprinkle with salt and pepper. Place on prepared broiler rack. Broil 5 inches from heat until instant-read thermometer inserted into side of steak registers 145°F, about 5 minutes per side. Transfer to cutting board and let stand 10 minutes. Cut steak across grain into 12 slices.

Per serving (3 slices steak): 187 Cal, 5 g Total Fat, 2 g Sat Fat, 614 mg Sod, 8 g Total Carb, 4 g Sugar, 0 g Fib, 26 g Prot.

Kielbasa and lentil stew

Serves 4

French green lentils, also known as Le Puy green lentils, are grown in the volcanic soil of the Auvergne region in France, which accounts for their unique nutty flavor.

1	**tbsp olive oil, divided**
¾	**lb turkey kielbasa, cut into 1-inch chunks**
1	**onion, thinly sliced**
1	**(14½-oz) can diced tomatoes with Italian herbs**
1	**cup water**
1	**(15-oz) can green lentils, drained, or 1½ cups vacuum-packed cooked green or brown lentils**
¼	**tsp salt**
⅛	**tsp black pepper**

1 Heat 2 tsp oil in a Dutch oven over medium-high heat. Add kielbasa and cook, stirring, until browned, about 5 minutes. With a slotted spoon, transfer kielbasa to plate and set aside.

2 Heat remaining 1 tsp oil in same saucepan. Add onion and cook, stirring occasionally, until golden, about 8 minutes. Reduce heat to medium and add tomatoes. Pour water into empty tomato can and swirl can, then add tomato water to saucepan along with lentils, salt, and pepper. Bring to simmer and cook, covered, 10 minutes.

3 Stir kielbasa into lentil mixture and simmer, uncovered, until heated through and flavors are blended, about 5 minutes.

Per serving (1¼ cups): 282 Cal, 11 g Total Fat, 3 g Sat Fat, 992 mg Sod, 25 g Total Carb, 5 g Sugar, 8 g Fib, 20 g Prot.

Kielbasa and
lentil stew

Coffee and chili–crusted tenderloin

Coffee and chili-crusted tenderloin

Serves 4

Who doesn't like a nice thick slice or two of tender, juicy beef tenderloin, especially when it's been coated with a tasty layer of flavor? Here, a dry rub of espresso powder, paprika, chili powder, salt, and pepper plays nicely against a thin layer of piquant Dijon.

1	**tbsp olive oil**
1	**(1½-lb) lean beef tenderloin, trimmed and tied**
1	**tbsp instant espresso powder, such as Medaglia d'Oro**
1½	**tsp paprika**
¾	**tsp chili powder**
½	**tsp salt**
½	**tsp black pepper**
2½	**tsp Dijon mustard**

1 Preheat oven to 425°F.

2 In a medium ovenproof skillet or heavy flameproof roasting pan over medium-high heat, warm oil. Add beef and cook, turning, until browned on all sides, 4 to 5 minutes. Transfer beef to a cutting board and let cool slightly. Remove string and discard. Set skillet aside (no need to wash).

3 Mix together espresso powder, paprika, chili powder, salt, and pepper in cup. Brush mustard all over beef but not on ends. Sprinkle two-thirds of coffee mixture over mustard, gently patting so it adheres. Sprinkle beef with remaining coffee mixture.

4 Return beef to skillet and roast in oven until instant-read thermometer inserted into center of beef registers 145°F, about 25 minutes. Transfer beef to cutting board, cover loosely with foil, and let stand 10 minutes. Cut into 8 thick slices and serve drizzled with any accumulated meat juices.

Per serving (2 slices tenderloin): 288 Cal, 14 g Total Fat, 4 g Sat Fat, 435 mg Sod, 1 g Total Carb, 0 g Sugar, 1 g Fib, 38 g Prot.

Braised Italian-style pork chops

Serves 4

1   **tbsp olive oil**

4   **(¼-lb) lean boneless center-cut pork loin chops, trimmed**

¾   **tsp salt**

¼   **tsp black pepper**

1   **onion, chopped**

1   **red or green bell pepper, diced**

2   **large garlic cloves, thinly sliced**

1   **cup spicy tomato sauce, such as arrabiatta**

1 In a large heavy nonstick skillet over medium-high heat, warm oil. Sprinkle pork with salt and black pepper and place in skillet. Cook until browned, about 3 minutes per side. Transfer to a plate.

2 Reduce heat to medium. Add onion, bell pepper, and garlic to skillet and cook, stirring, until vegetables begin to soften, about 3 minutes. Return pork chops to skillet and pour tomato sauce over. Simmer, covered, until an instant-read thermometer inserted into side of chop registers 145°F, about 5 minutes.

Per serving (1 pork chop and ⅔ cup sauce): 258 Cal, 13 g Total Fat, 3 g Sat Fat, 720 mg Sod, 9 g Total Carb, 5 g Sugar, 2 g Fib, 25 g Prot.

Add this

Grilled slices of unpeeled eggplant would play nicely with the flavors of this dish. And there's enough tomato sauce for spooning over the eggplant if you like.

Grilled Swiss chard and tomato pizzas

Serves 8

Olive-oil nonstick spray

1 **(¾-lb) bunch Swiss chard, tough stems removed and leaves cut into large pieces**

1 **red onion, cut into ¼-inch rounds**

1 **lb refrigerated pizza dough, at room temperature**

4 **large plum tomatoes, cut crosswise into ¼-inch slices**

¼ **tsp black pepper**

1 **cup shredded part-skim mozzarella**

1 Spray grill rack with nonstick spray. Preheat grill to medium-high or prepare medium-high fire.

2 Spray Swiss chard and onion with nonstick spray and place on grill rack. Grill, turning, until vegetables are lightly browned and tender, about 3 minutes for chard and 5 minutes for onion. Transfer vegetables to cutting board as they are done; coarsely chop. Keep grill on.

3 Divide dough into 4 equal pieces. On a lightly floured work surface with floured rolling pin, roll each piece of dough into thin round. Lightly spray tops of dough rounds with nonstick spray. Place dough rounds, sprayed-side down, on grill rack and grill until golden brown on bottom, about 2 minutes.

4 With tongs, transfer pizza crusts to cutting board or baking peel and turn cooked-side up. Spray crusts with nonstick spray and top evenly with chard, onion, and tomatoes; sprinkle with pepper and top with mozzarella. Return pizzas to grill and grill, covered, until golden brown on bottom and cheese has melted, about 3 minutes. Cut each pizza in half.

Per serving (½ pizza): 221 Cal, 7 g Total Fat, 3 g Sat Fat, 564 mg Sod, 29 g Total Carb, 5 g Sugar, 1 g Fib, 11 g Prot.

Cherry and thyme-stuffed pork

Serves 8

Serve this elegant yet easy-to-prepare pork roast the next time you want to dazzle guests. The roast can be stuffed and refrigerated up to 6 hours ahead. Leave it out at room temperature about 20 minutes before roasting.

Nonstick spray

⅓ **cup dried cherries, chopped**

½ **cup cherry all-fruit spread**

3 **tbsp plain dried bread crumbs**

4 **tsp chopped thyme**

1 **(1½-lb) lean boneless center-cut pork loin, trimmed**

¾ **tsp salt**

¼ **tsp black pepper**

1 Preheat oven to 400°F. Set rack in a roasting pan and spray rack and pan with nonstick spray.

2 To make stuffing: In a small bowl, combine cherries with enough boiling water to cover. Let cherries soak until softened, about 10 minutes; drain well. Stir in ¼ cup fruit spread, bread crumbs, and thyme until mixed well.

3 With long thin knife, cut pork lengthwise in half, cutting about three-fourths through and opening pork up like a book. Place pork, cut-side down, between two sheets of wax paper. With a meat mallet or rolling pin, gently pound pork to ½-inch thickness. Remove top sheet of wax paper and sprinkle pork with salt and pepper. Turn pork over and spoon cherry mixture down along center. Roll pork up lengthwise to enclose filling and tie in 4 or 5 places with kitchen string.

4 Place pork on prepared rack and roast 45 minutes Brush with 1 tbsp of fruit spread. Roast until instant-read thermometer inserted into center of pork registers 145°F, about 15 minutes longer, brushing 3 times with remaining fruit spread. Transfer pork to cutting board and let stand 10 minutes. Cut off string and discard. Cut pork into 24 (¼-inch) slices.

Per serving (3 slices pork): 163 Cal, 4 g Total Fat, 2 g Sat Fat, 292 mg Sod, 13 g Total Carb, 6 g Sugar, 4 g Fib, 19 g Prot.

Cherry and
thyme-stuffed pork

Butterflied lamb with couscous salad

Serves 4

This recipe showcases the delicate flavor of spring lamb. Give the grill pan enough time to get good and hot, ensuring the lamb gets a crust on the outside while remaining tender and juicy on the inside.

Nonstick spray
1   **cup whole-wheat couscous**
1   **tbsp extra-virgin olive oil**
1   **tomato, cut into small dice**
⅓   **cup chopped flat-leaf parsley**
1½ **tsp salt, divided**
½   **tsp black pepper, divided**
1   **(1-lb) lean boneless leg of lamb, butterflied and trimmed**

1 Cook couscous according to package directions. Transfer to a serving bowl and let cool slightly; fluff with fork. Drizzle with oil and stir in tomato, parsley, ½ tsp of salt, and ¼ tsp of pepper.

2 Meanwhile, spray a ridged grill pan with nonstick spray and set over medium-high heat until hot. Sprinkle lamb with remaining 1 tsp salt and ¼ tsp pepper. Place lamb in pan and cook, turning once, until instant-read thermometer inserted into center of lamb registers 145°F, about 12 minutes.

3 Transfer lamb to cutting board and let stand 10 minutes. Cut across grain into 12 slices. Serve with couscous.

Per serving (3 slices lamb and about 1 cup couscous): 334 Cal, 8 g Total Fat, 2 g Sat Fat, 968 mg Sod, 35 g Total Carb, 4 g Sugar, 6 g Fib, 30 g Prot.

Serving idea
Make our tasty, easy Lemony Fennel and Radicchio (page 137) alongside this dish.

Butterflied
lamb with
couscous salad

Spaghettini with limas and tomatoes

Serves 4

In the spring, make this dish even more delicious by substituting fresh fava beans for the lima beans. To get 2 cups beans you'll need about 2 lb pods.

1	tbsp extra-virgin olive oil
2	(14½-oz) cans diced fire-roasted tomatoes with garlic
2	cups frozen baby lima beans
½	tsp black pepper
½	lb spaghettini (thin spaghetti)
⅔	cup torn basil leaves

1 In a large deep skillet over medium-high heat, warm oil. Add tomatoes, lima beans, and pepper and bring to a boil. Reduce heat and simmer, covered, stirring occasionally, 20 minutes.

2 Meanwhile, cook spaghettini according to package directions. Drain spaghettini and add to tomato mixture, tossing until mixed. Transfer to a serving bowl. Add basil and toss until combined.

Per serving (1½ cups): 385 Cal, 5 g Total Fat, 1 g Sat Fat, 333 mg Sod, 70 g Total Carb, 8 g Sugar, 9 g Fib, 15 g Prot.

Try this
Begin your meal with a mixed baby greens salad dressed with fresh lemon juice, salt, and pepper.

Stir-fried tofu with scallions

Serves 4

Tofu is akin to a sponge, as it happily absorbs the flavors of other ingredients. Since tofu is so mild-flavored, tossing it with black bean sauce, which has a complex flavor profile, works like a charm.

1	**(14-oz) package extra-firm tofu, drained**
2	**bunches small scallions (white and light green parts only), trimmed**
2	**tsp canola oil**
¼	**tsp black pepper, divided**
2	**tsp dark sesame oil**
2	**orange bell peppers, cut into 1-inch pieces**
⅓	**cup water**
⅓	**cup black bean sauce**

1 Gently press tofu between several layers of paper towels to remove excess water. Cut into 1-inch cubes. Set aside.

2 Cut 2 scallions lengthwise in half and then into long, thin shreds. Set aside. Cut remaining scallions crosswise into thirds. Set aside.

3 Heat a wok or large heavy deep nonstick skillet over medium-high heat until a drop of water sizzles in wok. Add canola oil, swirling to coat pan. Add tofu, sprinkle with ⅛ tsp black pepper and cook, turning tofu occasionally, until golden, about 5 minutes. Transfer to plate.

4 Increase heat to high. Add sesame oil to wok along with bell peppers, scallion pieces, and remaining ⅛ tsp black pepper. Stir-fry until bell peppers are lightly charred, about 4 minutes. Reduce heat to low and stir in water and black bean sauce. Cook, stirring, until heated through, about 2 minutes. Gently stir in tofu and shredded scallions.

Per serving (about 1 cup): 201 Cal, 12 g Total Fat, 2 g Sat Fat, 481 mg Sod, 12 g Total Carb, 4 g Sugar, 4 g Fib, 14 g Prot.

Polenta "pizza" margherita

Serves 4

Creamy, rich ricotta is unusual in that it is made from the whey leftover from cheese making.

Nonstick spray

1 **(1-lb) tube plain fat-free polenta, cut into ¼-inch rounds**

¾ **cup part-skim ricotta**

¼ **cup grated Parmesan**

¼ **tsp black pepper**

3 **plum tomatoes, thinly sliced into rounds and patted dry with paper towels**

½ **cup shredded part-skim mozzarella**

1 Preheat broiler. Spray a 10-inch pizza pan or large baking sheet with nonstick spray.

2 Place 1 slice of polenta in center of prepared pan. Arrange remaining slices of polenta in two concentric circles around first slice, slightly overlapping polenta to form 10-inch polenta round. Lightly spray polenta with nonstick spray. Broil 5 inches from heat until lightly browned and heated through, about 8 minutes.

3 Meanwhile, in a small bowl, stir together ricotta, Parmesan, and pepper.

4 Arrange tomato slices on top of polenta and dollop with ricotta-Parmesan mixture; sprinkle with mozzarella. Broil until tomatoes are heated through and mozzarella has melted, about 4 minutes. Cut into 4 wedges.

Per serving (1 wedge): 214 Cal, 8 g Total Fat, 5 g Sat Fat, 577 mg Sod, 22 g Total Carb, 2 g Sugar, 2 g Fib, 13 g Prot.

Polenta "pizza" margherita

Marinated tofu and vegetable kebabs

Marinated tofu and vegetable kebabs

Serves 4

Nonstick spray

1   **(14-oz) package extra-firm tofu, drained**

2   **zucchini, each cut into 12 (½-inch) slices**

1   **red bell pepper, cut into 1-inch pieces**

1   **red onion, quartered and separated into 16 pieces**

¼   **cup teriyaki sauce**

⅛   **tsp black pepper**

1 Line a broiler pan with foil and spray broiler rack with nonstick spray.

2 Gently press tofu between several layers of paper towels to remove excess water. Cut into 24 (1-inch) cubes.

3 Thread tofu alternately with zucchini, bell pepper, and onion onto 8 (10- to 12-inch) metal skewers (if using wooden skewers, soak them in water at least 20 minutes to prevent charring).

4 Place skewers on a baking sheet. Brush on all sides with some teriyaki sauce. Let stand about 30 minutes, turning and brushing with sauce once or twice more.

5 Meanwhile, preheat broiler to high.

6 Transfer kebabs to prepared broiler rack. Broil about 4 inches from heat, turning several times, until vegetables have started to soften and tofu has browned, about 12 minutes. Sprinkle with black pepper.

Per serving (2 kebabs): 147 Cal, 6 g Total Fat, 1 g Sat Fat, 703 mg Sod, 13 g Total Carb, 7 g Sugar, 4 g Fib, 14 g Prot.

Serving idea
Put the cooked tofu and vegetables onto Boston lettuce leaves and enjoy as wraps.

Chapter 5
Eat your "greens"

Roasted Brussels sprouts with walnuts, 122

Sesame broccoli, 124

Braised red cabbage and pears, 125

Very French grated carrot salad, 127

Carrot–horseradish puree, 128

Cauliflower with lemon and cumin, 129

Whole roasted tandoori cauliflower, 131

Grilled Parmesan corn on the cob, 132

"Creamed" corn, 134

Coconut-cumin green beans, 135

Lemony fennel and radicchio, 137

Peas with crispy prosciutto, 139

Rosemary-roasted radishes, 141

Stir-fried garlic spinach, 142

Roasted acorn squash with thyme, 143

Tomato and garlic–stuffed peppers, 144

Quick-cook fresh tomato sauce, 146

Grilled zucchini with feta and lemon, 147

Three-vegetable tian, 149

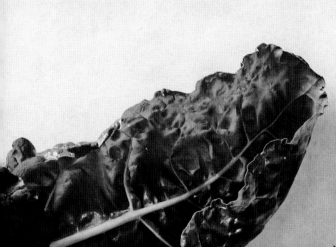

Roasted Brussels sprouts with walnuts

Serves 8

Tender sweet shallots and perfectly cooked Brussels sprouts are a welcome texture counterpoint to the crunchy toasted walnuts.

2	**pints Brussels sprouts, trimmed and halved or quartered if large**
4	**large shallots, thickly sliced**
2	**tbsp olive oil**
½	**tsp salt**
¼	**tsp black pepper**
4	**slices center-cut bacon, crisp-cooked and torn into ½-inch pieces**
¼	**cup walnuts, chopped and toasted**

1 Preheat oven to 450°F.

2 Combine Brussels sprouts and shallots on a large rimmed baking sheet. Drizzle with oil and sprinkle with salt and pepper, tossing until coated evenly. Spread to form even layer. Roast until Brussels sprouts and shallots are tender, about 20 minutes, stirring once or twice.

3 Transfer Brussels sprouts mixture to a serving bowl. Add bacon and walnuts and toss until mixed well.

Per serving (½ cup): 118 Cal, 8 g Total Fat, 1 g Sat Fat, 256 mg Sod, 9 g Total Carb, 3 g Sugar, 3 g Fib, 5 g Prot.

**Roasted Brussels sprouts
with walnuts**

Sesame broccoli

Serves 4

This recipe is delicious as is, but if you want a flavorful vegetable to add, try red bell peppers, which are high in vitamin C. Thinly slice a large red bell pepper and add it to the steamer basket along with the broccoli in step 1.

4	**cups small broccoli florets**
2	**tbsp soy sauce**
1	**tbsp honey**
2	**tsp dark sesame oil**
2	**tsp toasted sesame seeds**
1	**garlic clove, crushed through a press**

1 Put broccoli in a steamer basket set in a large saucepan over 1 inch of boiling water. Cover and steam until broccoli is crisp-tender, about 4 minutes.

2 Meanwhile, in a serving bowl, stir together soy sauce, honey, sesame oil, sesame seeds, and garlic. Add broccoli and toss until mixed well.

Per serving (1 cup): 70 Cal, 3 g Total Fat, 0 g Sat Fat, 455 mg Sod, 9 g Total Carb, 5 g Sugar, 2 g Fib, 3 g Prot.

Braised red cabbage and pears

Serves 6

Order a side of *blaukraut* in a German or German-American restaurant and you'll get a bowl of braised red cabbage. Meltingly tender with a subtle sweet-and-sour edge, it's the perfect hearty accompaniment to game, poultry, or pork.

1	**small red cabbage (about 1½ lb), quartered, cored, and thinly sliced**
2	**ripe Bosc or Bartlett pears, peeled, cored, quartered, and thickly sliced crosswise**
1	**small onion, thinly sliced**
2	**tbsp cider vinegar**
2	**tbsp water**
½	**tsp salt**
¼	**tsp black pepper**
1	**tbsp unsalted butter, cut into small pieces**

1 Combine cabbage, pears, onion, vinegar, water, salt, and pepper in a large pot and set over medium heat. Cook, covered, until cabbage is wilted, about 10 minutes.

2 Reduce heat to medium-low and cook, stirring occasionally, until cabbage is very tender, about 30 minutes, adding a couple tbsp of water if mixture seems dry. Stir in butter until melted.

Per serving (¾ cup): 89 Cal, 2 g Total Fat, 1 g Sat Fat, 222 mg Sod, 18 g Total Carb, 10 g Sugar, 4 g Fib, 2 g Prot.

Serving idea
Pair this delicious sweet-and-sour braised cabbage with grilled or broiled skinless boneless chicken breasts or salmon fillets; however, the recipe will no longer be vegetarian.

Very French grated carrot salad

Very French grated carrot salad

Serves 4

Carrot salad, *carottes rapées,* can be found in just about every take-out shop in France. The key to success is laying the carrots on their sides and using the thinnest shredding blade your food processor has.

¾ **lb large carrots**

1 **tbsp finely chopped flat-leaf parsley**

1 **tbsp lemon juice**

2 **tsp Dijon mustard**

¼ **tsp salt**

⅛ **tsp black pepper**

1 **tbsp plus 1 tsp extra-virgin olive oil**

1 Cut carrots to fit horizontally in the feed tube of a food processor. Stack carrots in feed tube and grate using thin shredding blade (or use large holes of box grater) to create long, thin strands (you need about 3 cups). Transfer carrots to salad bowl and add parsley.

2 To make dressing: In a small bowl, whisk together lemon juice, mustard, salt, and pepper. Slowly whisk in oil in thin, steady steam.

3 Pour dressing over carrot mixture and toss until mixed well. Let stand, covered, at room temperature up to 3 hours.

Per serving (½ cup): 77 Cal, 5 g Total Fat, 1 g Sat Fat, 232 mg Sod, 9 g Total Carb, 4 g Sugar, 2 g Fib, 1 g Prot.

Carrot-horseradish puree

Serves 4

Here carrots are cooked until tender then whirled in a food processor until silky smooth. Butter adds a touch of creamy richness, while bottled horseradish gives it an unexpected note of heat. Serve this at your next Thanksgiving dinner.

1½	**lb carrots, very thinly sliced**
1	**tbsp reduced-fat (2%) milk**
1	**tbsp butter**
1	**tbsp prepared horseradish**
½	**tsp salt (or to taste)**
¼	**tsp black pepper**

1 Bring a large saucepan of water to a boil. Add carrots and return to a boil. Reduce heat and simmer, covered, until carrots are very tender, about 15 minutes. Drain well.

2 Combine carrots, milk, and butter in a food processor and process until very smooth. Transfer to a serving bowl and stir in horseradish, salt, and pepper.

Per serving (about ½ cup): 51 Cal, 3 g Total Fat, 2 g Sat Fat, 346 mg Sod, 6 g Total Carb, 3 g Sugar, 2 g Fib, 1 g Prot.

Cauliflower with lemon and cumin

Serves 4

1	**small head cauliflower, cut into small florets**
2	**tsp olive oil**
½	**tsp ground cumin**
½	**tsp salt**
¼	**tsp black pepper**
	Grated zest and juice of ½ lemon
1	**garlic clove, minced**

1 Preheat oven to 450°F.

2 Put cauliflower on a large rimmed baking sheet. Drizzle with oil and sprinkle with cumin, salt, and pepper. Toss until coated evenly; spread to form even layer.

3 Roast 15 minutes, stirring once. Sprinkle cauliflower with lemon zest and juice and garlic, tossing to coat. Roast until cauliflower is tender, about 3 minutes longer.

Per serving (1 cup): 42 Cal, 2 g Total Fat, 0 g Sat Fat, 312 mg Sod, 5 g Total Carb, 2 g Sugar, 2 g Fib, 2 g Prot.

Try this

Our vegetable side dish, brightly flavored with lemon juice and zest, would pair well with grilled or broiled chicken breasts, salmon steaks, shrimp, or calamari.

Whole roasted
tandoori cauliflower

Whole roasted tandoori cauliflower

Serves 6

Don't tell anyone how easy it was to prepare this vegetable showstopper! Brilliant yellow on the outside and perfectly tender on the inside, cauliflower never tasted this good. If you'd like, roast it up to several hours ahead, then reheat in the microwave.

Nonstick spray
1   **large head cauliflower**
⅔   **cup plain fat-free Greek yogurt**
2   **garlic cloves, minced**
1½   **tsp tandoori seasoning**
½   **tsp salt**
2   **tbsp chopped cilantro**

1 Preheat oven to 400°F. Spray a 9-inch pie plate or small shallow baking dish with nonstick spray.

2 Remove outer leaves and core from cauliflower and discard, keeping head intact. Place cauliflower in prepared baking dish, core-side down. In a small bowl, whisk together yogurt, garlic, tandoori seasoning, and salt. Spread evenly over cauliflower.

3 Roast until small knife inserted into center of cauliflower goes in easily and topping is browned, about 1 hour 30 minutes, rotating dish once or twice during roasting so cauliflower cooks evenly.

4 Let cauliflower stand 10 minutes to cool slightly. Sprinkle with cilantro and cut into 6 wedges.

Per serving (1 wedge): 52 Cal, 0 g Total Fat, 0 g Sat Fat, 249 mg Sod, 9 g Total Carb, 4 g Sugar, 4 g Fib, 5 g Prot.

Grilled Parmesan corn on the cob

Serves 8

This classic Mexican street food can take the heat. Add 1 or 2 tsp of chili powder (pictured) or a pinch of cayenne to the mayonnaise mixture.

8 ears of corn

⅔ cup reduced-fat mayonnaise

¼ cup chopped cilantro

Grated zest and juice of 1 lime

¼ cup grated Parmesan

1 Preheat grill to medium-high or prepare medium-high fire.

2 Gently pull husks down from corn and remove silk. Pull husks back over corn.

3 Wrap each ear of corn in a sheet of heavy foil. Place on grill rack and grill, turning corn occasionally, until very tender, about 15 minutes.

4 Meanwhile, mix together mayonnaise, cilantro, and lime zest and juice in a cup.

5 Remove husks from corn, brush all over with mayonnaise mixture, and sprinkle with Parmesan.

Per serving (1 ear of corn): 162 Cal, 7 g Total Fat, 1 g Sat Fat, 223 mg Sod, 25 g Total Carb, 6 g Sugar, 3 g Fib, 5 g Prot.

Grilled Parmesan
corn on the cob

"Creamed" corn

Serves 4

Typically, creamed corn is made by cooking corn kernels with a little sugar and a good amount of heavy cream. But if you grate the corn from some of the ears, you end up with creamed corn that is laden with fresh corn flavor.

6	**ears of corn, husks and silk removed**
2	**tsp olive oil**
1	**small onion, finely chopped**
½	**cup vegetable broth**
¼	**tsp salt**
⅛	**tsp black pepper**
1	**tbsp water**
2	**tsp cornstarch**

1 Hold a box grater over a large bowl, and using large holes, grate corn from 4 ears, letting milky liquid fall into bowl. Standing remaining ears of corn, one at a time, on cutting board, slice down length of ears to remove corn, cutting as close to cob as possible. Coarsely chop kernels and stir into corn liquid. Set aside.

2 In a medium saucepan over medium heat, warm oil. Add onion and cook, stirring, until softened, about 5 minutes. Stir in corn mixture, broth, salt, and pepper and bring to a boil. Reduce heat and simmer, covered, stirring occasionally, until corn is tender, about 10 minutes.

3 Meanwhile, whisk together water and cornstarch in a cup until smooth. Stir into corn and cook, stirring constantly, until mixture is slightly thickened, about 1 minute.

Per serving (about ¾ cup): 181 Cal, 5 g Total Fat, 1 g Sat Fat, 231 mg Sod, 36 g Total Carb, 8 g Sugar, 4 g Fib, 6 g Prot.

Coconut-cumin green beans

Serves 4

Did you know that green beans are also called snap beans? This well-deserved name reflects the sound the beans make when their ends are snapped (broken) off to trim them.

1	**lb green beans, trimmed**
2	**tsp canola oil**
⅓	**cup unsweetened flaked coconut**
½	**tsp cumin seeds, crushed**
½	**tsp salt**
⅛	**tsp black pepper**

1 Bring a medium saucepan of water to a boil over high heat. Add green beans and cook, covered, until crisp-tender, about 3 minutes. Drain and cover to keep warm.

2 Meanwhile, heat oil in a large skillet over medium heat. Add coconut and cumin and cook, stirring constantly, until coconut is toasted, about 2 minutes. Add green beans, salt, and pepper and cook, stirring constantly, until heated through, about 1 minute longer.

Per serving (generous ¾ cup): 87 Cal, 5 g Total Fat, 3 g Sat Fat, 304 mg Sod, 9 g Total Carb, 2 g Sugar, 5 g Fib, 2 g Prot.

**Lemony fennel
and radicchio**

Lemony fennel and radicchio

Serves 4

Italians love their fennel for its anise (licorice) flavor. Also known as Florence fennel and finocchio, it is as much at home in salads as it is roasted, braised, or grilled. If the fennel comes with its feathery fronds, chop them and scatter over the finished dish.

2	**fennel bulbs, trimmed and thinly sliced lengthwise**
1	**tbsp olive oil**
¼	**tsp salt**
⅛	**tsp black pepper**
¼	**cup water**
1	**cup thinly sliced radicchio**
2	**tbsp chopped flat-leaf parsley**
1	**tsp grated lemon zest**
1	**tbsp lemon juice**

1 Put fennel in a large bowl. Add oil and toss until coated evenly. Transfer fennel to a large nonstick skillet; sprinkle with salt and pepper and set over medium heat. Cook, stirring, 1 minute. Add water and cook, covered, until fennel begins to soften, about 3 minutes longer.

2 Uncover skillet and increase heat to medium-high. Cook, stirring, until most of water has evaporated and fennel is tender, about 2 minutes. Remove skillet from heat and stir in radicchio, parsley, and lemon zest and juice.

Per serving (1 cup): 71 Cal, 4 g Total Fat, 0 g Sat Fat, 210 mg Sod, 10 g Total Carb, 0 g Sugar, 4 g Fib, 2 g Prot.

**Peas with
crispy prosciutto**

Peas with crispy prosciutto

Serves 4

2   tsp olive oil, divided

2   (½-oz) slices prosciutto, trimmed and torn into small pieces or chopped

1   large shallot, halved lengthwise and thinly sliced

2½   cups frozen peas (about 12 oz)

⅓   cup water

⅛   tsp salt

⅛   tsp black pepper

1   tbsp thinly sliced mint

1 Heat 1 tsp oil in a medium heavy nonstick skillet over medium-high heat. Add prosciutto and cook, stirring often, until crisp, about 3 minutes. With a slotted spoon, transfer prosciutto to paper towels to drain.

2 Add remaining 1 tsp oil to skillet. Add shallot and cook, stirring, until softened but not browned, about 2 minutes. Stir in peas, water, salt, and pepper and bring to a boil. Reduce heat and simmer until peas are tender and most of water has evaporated, about 4 minutes.

3 Remove skillet from heat and stir in mint. Transfer to serving bowl and crumble prosciutto on top.

Per serving (about ½ cup): 125 Cal, 4 g Total Fat, 1 g Sat Fat, 414 mg Sod, 15 g Total Carb, 6 g Sugar, 5 g Fib, 8 g Prot.

**Rosemary-roasted
radishes**

Rosemary-roasted radishes

Serves 4

The green tops of radishes are a welcome change from other more common greens. Firm textured with a slight bite, they are a good-for-you veggie that tastes great cooked as well as raw in a salad.

2	**large bunches of radishes with green tops attached (about 20)**
1	**tbsp olive oil**
2	**tsp chopped rosemary**
½	**tsp salt**
¼	**tsp black pepper**
1	**tsp lemon juice**

1 Set rack in upper third of oven. Preheat oven to 425°F.

2 Separate radishes and green tops; set greens aside. Trim radishes and cut lengthwise in half.

3 In a large bowl, combine radishes, oil, rosemary, salt, and pepper, tossing until coated. Transfer to a large rimmed baking sheet, leaving about 1 tsp rosemary mixture in bowl. Roast radishes 20 minutes.

4 Meanwhile, rinse radish greens under cool water to remove any grit or sand, discarding any wilted or yellowing leaves. Tear any large leaves in half and trim any tough stems. Add greens to rosemary mixture in bowl and toss until coated. Remove radishes from oven and add greens, tossing until combined. Roast until greens are wilted and radishes are tender, about 5 minutes. Drizzle with lemon juice.

Per serving (generous ⅔ cup): 38 Cal, 3 g Total Fat, 0 g Sat Fat, 308 mg Sod, 2 g Total Carb, 1 g Sugar, 1 g Fib, 0 g Prot.

Stir-fried garlic spinach

Serves 4

There are three types of spinach in supermarkets: baby spinach, curly spinach, and flat spinach, which is sold by the bunch. Flat spinach is more delicate than curly spinach and not as pricey as baby spinach, making it a great choice.

2	tsp canola oil
2	large garlic cloves, minced
10	oz flat spinach, trimmed
1	tbsp soy sauce
1	tbsp rice vinegar
⅛	tsp black pepper

Heat a wok or large heavy deep nonstick skillet over high heat until a drop of water sizzles in wok. Add oil and swirl to coat pan. Add garlic and stir-fry just until fragrant, about 15 seconds. Add spinach, soy sauce, vinegar, and pepper and stir-fry just until spinach is wilted, about 2 minutes.

Per serving (about ⅓ cup): 42 Cal, 3 g Total Fat, 0 g Sat Fat, 274 mg Sod, 4 g Total Carb, 0 g Sugar, 2 g Fib, 2 g Prot.

Roasted acorn squash with thyme

Serves 4

Olive-oil nonstick spray

2 acorn squash

1 tbsp olive oil

1½ tbsp chopped thyme

½ tsp kosher salt

¼ tsp black pepper

1 Preheat oven to 400°F. Spray a large rimmed baking sheet with nonstick spray.

2 Using a long serrated knife, halve squash through stem end. With spoon, scrape out seeds and cut each squash half in half to make total of 8 wedges. Place squash, skin-side down, on prepared baking sheet. Brush with oil and sprinkle with thyme, salt, and pepper.

3 Roast until squash is tender and golden brown along edges, about 40 minutes.

Per serving (2 wedges): 118 Cal, 4 g Total Fat, 1 g Sat Fat, 248 mg Sod, 23 g Total Carb, 0 g Sugar, 3 g Fib, 2 g Prot.

Try this

Roasted acorn squash is a made-for-fall vegetable. Enjoy it at your next Thanksgiving dinner. The recipe is easily doubled or even tripled. Roast the squash, in batches if needed, early in the day, and re-warm in a 200°F oven once you've taken out the turkey.

Tomato and garlic-stuffed peppers

Serves 4

Pretty as a picture and as flavorful as can be, these hardly-any-fuss stuffed peppers are sure to become part of your go-to recipe repertoire. Get creative and use assorted-color peppers, such as orange, yellow, purple, or green, for a carnival of colors.

Nonstick spray

4 red bell peppers

48 cherry tomatoes (about 1½ lb)

2 garlic cloves, thinly sliced

3 anchovies (packed in oil), thinly sliced and 2½ tsp oil reserved

2 large rosemary or thyme sprigs

⅛ tsp salt

⅛ tsp black pepper

1 Preheat oven to 375°F. Line a large rimmed baking sheet with foil and spray with nonstick spray.

2 Cut bell peppers lengthwise in half being sure to cut through middle of each stem to keep intact. Carefully remove cores and seeds and discard. Place peppers, cut-side up, on prepared baking sheet.

3 Tightly fit about 6 whole cherry tomatoes into each pepper half. Tuck garlic and anchovies into each half, dividing evenly. Break rosemary sprigs into little sprigs and tuck between tomatoes. Drizzle reserved anchovy oil over tomatoes and sprinkle with salt and pepper.

4 Roast until bell peppers are tender and browned along edges and tomatoes are softened, about 40 minutes.

Per serving (2 stuffed pepper halves): 86 Cal, 4 g Total Fat, 1 g Sat Fat, 192 mg Sod, 12 g Total Carb, 7 g Sugar, 4 g Fib, 3 g Prot.

Tomato and garlic-stuffed peppers

Quick-cook fresh tomato sauce

Serves 8

Got an abundance of tomatoes in your garden? Pick the ripest ones you can find and use them here. Sauce made with fresh tomatoes has a delicate flavor, which is especially welcome during the warmer months.

3	**tbsp olive oil**
1	**small onion, chopped**
4	**large garlic cloves**
2	**lb ripe tomatoes, cored and diced, juice reserved**
1	**tbsp tomato paste**
2	**tsp kosher salt**
¼	**tsp black pepper**
½	**cup chopped basil**

1 In a large saucepan over medium heat, warm oil. Add onion and cook, stirring, until softened, about 5 minutes. Add garlic and cook, stirring frequently, until fragrant, about 30 seconds.

2 Add tomatoes with their juice, tomato paste, salt, and pepper; cook, stirring, until tomatoes break down and begin to soften, about 4 minutes. Stir in basil.

Per serving (½ cup): 73 Cal, 5 g Total Fat, 1 g Sat Fat, 505 mg Sod, 6 g Total Carb, 4 g Sugar, 2 g Fib, 1 g Prot.

Grilled zucchini with feta and lemon

Serves 6

Take advantage of the abundance and low price of zucchini at the height of summer in your local farmers' market. This easy dish is great for serving a crowd.

Nonstick spray

½ **cup crumbled reduced-fat feta**

3 **scallions, thinly sliced**

1 **tbsp extra-virgin olive oil**

Grated zest of 1 lemon

4 **(6-oz) zucchini, ends trimmed**

½ **tsp kosher salt**

¼ **tsp black pepper**

1 Spray grill rack with nonstick spray. Preheat grill to high or prepare hot fire.

2 Meanwhile, in a small bowl, stir together feta, scallions, oil, and lemon zest; set aside.

3 Cut zucchini lengthwise in half and cut each half into 4 or 5 pieces. Put zucchini into large bowl and lightly spray with nonstick spray. Sprinkle with salt and pepper, tossing to coat.

4 Place zucchini on grill rack and grill, turning, until well-marked and tender, about 6 minutes. Transfer zucchini to a platter or serving bowl and sprinkle with feta mixture.

Per serving (about 5 pieces zucchini and heaping 1 tbsp feta mixture): 63 Cal, 4 g Total Fat, 1 g Sat Fat, 294 mg Sod, 53 g Total Carb, 3 g Sugar, 1 g Fib, 4 g Prot.

Add this
A small handful of thinly sliced or torn mint leaves would make a flavorful addition to this tasty vegetable dish.

Three-vegetable tian

Three-vegetable tian

Serves 4

Olive-oil nonstick spray	
4	small thyme sprigs plus 1½ tsp finely chopped thyme
2	tbsp plus 1 tsp extra-virgin olive oil
2	(5-oz) evenly shaped slender eggplant, trimmed and cut into ¼-inch rounds
3	(¼-lb) plum tomatoes, cut into ¼-inch slices
1	large zucchini (about 10 oz), cut into ¼-inch slices
½	tsp salt
¼	tsp black pepper

1 Preheat oven to 400°F. Spray a 7½ x 10-inch rectangular or oval shallow baking dish with nonstick spray. Scatter thyme sprigs in bottom of dish.

2 Mix together oil and chopped thyme in a cup. Arrange eggplant, tomato, and zucchini slices in a single layer on a large baking sheet or on a large sheet of foil. Brush thyme oil over vegetables and sprinkle with salt and pepper.

3 Stand vegetables in tight rows in prepared baking dish, alternating vegetables. Spray with nonstick spray.

4 Bake until vegetables are tender and lightly browned along edges, about 50 minutes. Let stand at least 5 minutes to allow flavors to blend. Serve hot, warm, or at room temperature.

Per serving (¾ cup): 118 Cal, 9 g Total Fat, 1 g Sat Fat, 303 mg Sod, 10 g Total Carb, 6 g Sugar, 4 g Fib, 2 g Prot.

Chapter 6
Beans, roots, and grains

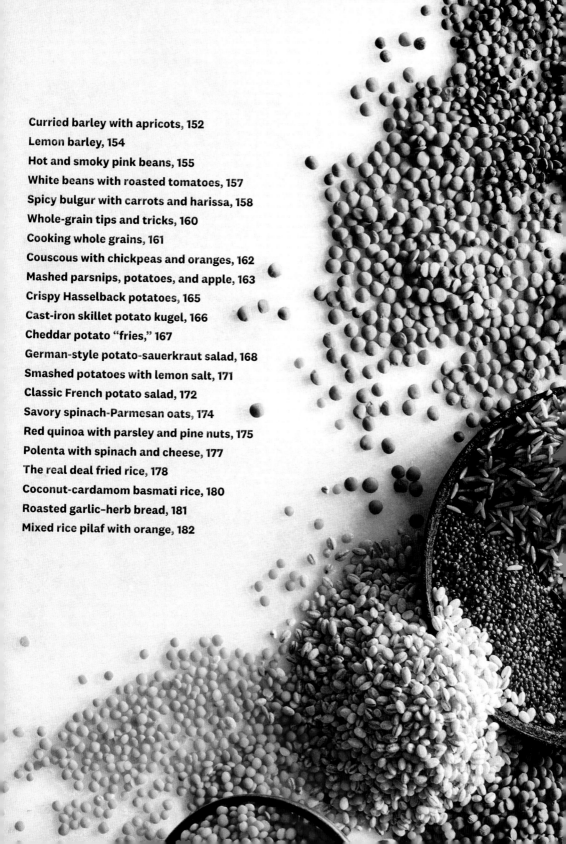

Curried barley with apricots, 152

Lemon barley, 154

Hot and smoky pink beans, 155

White beans with roasted tomatoes, 157

Spicy bulgur with carrots and harissa, 158

Whole-grain tips and tricks, 160

Cooking whole grains, 161

Couscous with chickpeas and oranges, 162

Mashed parsnips, potatoes, and apple, 163

Crispy Hasselback potatoes, 165

Cast-iron skillet potato kugel, 166

Cheddar potato "fries," 167

German-style potato-sauerkraut salad, 168

Smashed potatoes with lemon salt, 171

Classic French potato salad, 172

Savory spinach-Parmesan oats, 174

Red quinoa with parsley and pine nuts, 175

Polenta with spinach and cheese, 177

The real deal fried rice, 178

Coconut-cardamom basmati rice, 180

Roasted garlic–herb bread, 181

Mixed rice pilaf with orange, 182

Curried barley with apricots

Serves 6

Richly flavored dried apricots and bright green pistachio nuts are often combined, especially in Middle Eastern dishes. Here the barley is toasted to bring out its earthy flavor, while the addition of Madras curry powder adds a bit of the exotic.

Olive-oil nonstick spray

¾   **cup pearl barley**

1   **tbsp Madras curry powder, divided**

2½ **cups water**

¾   **tsp salt, divided**

2   **tsp olive oil**

1   **cup sliced scallions (about 4 large)**

¼   **cup pistachios, chopped**

3   **tbsp chopped dried apricots**

1 Spray a large heavy saucepan with nonstick spray and set over medium heat. Add barley and 2 tsp curry powder and cook, stirring frequently, until barley is lightly toasted and mixture is fragrant, about 5 minutes.

2 Add water and ½ tsp salt to saucepan and bring to a boil. Reduce heat and simmer, covered, until barley is tender, about 35 minutes. Drain off any excess liquid and transfer barley to serving bowl (no need to keep warm).

3 Heat oil in the same saucepan over medium heat. Add scallions and remaining 1 tsp curry powder and ¼ tsp salt and cook, stirring, until scallions are tender and mixture is fragrant, about 2 minutes.

4 Add scallion mixture, pistachios, and apricots to barley. Stir until mixed well.

Per serving (about ⅔ cup): 147 Cal, 4 g Total Fat, 1 g Sat Fat, 299 mg Sod, 25 g Total Carb, 3 g Sugar, 5 g Fib, 4 g Prot.

Add this
Tossing in chopped or torn mint leaves would add another layer of complexity. About ¼ cup would be the right amount.

Curried barley with apricots

Lemon barley

Serves 4

1⅓ cups water

½ tsp salt

⅔ cup quick-cooking barley

2 tsp olive oil

1 small onion, thinly sliced

1 zucchini, cut into ¼-inch dice

Grated zest of 1 large lemon

¼ tsp black pepper

1 In a medium saucepan, combine water, ¼ tsp of salt, and barley and bring to boil. Reduce heat and simmer, covered, until barley is tender, about 12 minutes.

2 Meanwhile, heat oil in a medium nonstick skillet over medium heat. Add onion and zucchini and cook, stirring, until onion is golden, about 8 minutes. Stir in barley, lemon zest, pepper, and remaining ¼ tsp salt. Cook, stirring, until heated through, about 2 minutes longer.

Per serving (scant 1 cup): 74 Cal, 3 g Total Fat, 0 g Sat Fat, 299 mg Sod, 13 g Total Carb, 3 g Sugar, 2 g Fib, 2 g Prot.

Hot and smoky pink beans

Serves 8

The time it takes for dried beans to cook depends on the type of bean, how old they are, and how long they have been soaked. It's a good idea to start checking the beans for doneness after about 50 minutes of cooking time.

½   lb dried pink beans,
     picked over and rinsed

2   tsp olive oil

1   onion, chopped

3   cups chicken broth

½   tsp salt

1½ tsp chipotles en
     adobo (or to taste), minced

1 Quick-soak beans according to package directions. Drain.

2 Heat oil in a medium saucepan over medium heat. Add onion and cook, stirring, until softened, about 5 minutes. Add broth and beans and bring to a boil. Reduce heat to low and simmer, covered, 40 minutes. Add salt and cook, uncovered, until beans are tender and still hold their shape, 20 to 40 minutes longer. Stir in chipotles en adobo.

Per serving (about ½ cup): 127 Cal, 2 g Total Fat, 0 g Sat Fat, 436 mg Sod, 20 g Total Carb, 1 g Sugar, 4 g Fib, 8 g Prot.

Try this
These delectably smoky beans would be the perfect side dish for grilled spice-rubbed skinless boneless chicken breasts.

White beans with roasted tomatoes

White beans with roasted tomatoes

Serves 4

This great-tasting Italian side dish can do double duty as the base for a non-vegetarian main that features a lean protein.

2 pints red and/or yellow grape tomatoes

1 tbsp extra-virgin olive oil, divided

1 tsp dried thyme

¾ tsp kosher or coarse sea salt, divided

¼ tsp black pepper, divided

1 large garlic clove, minced

2 cups canned white beans, rinsed and drained (from 19-oz can)

Scant ¼ cup sliced basil

1 Preheat oven to 400°F.

2 On a rimmed baking sheet, toss together tomatoes, 2 tsp oil, thyme, ½ tsp salt, and ⅛ tsp pepper. Roast until tomatoes collapse, 25 to 35 minutes.

3 About 5 minutes before tomatoes are done, heat remaining 1 tsp oil in a medium nonstick skillet over medium heat. Add garlic and cook, stirring, until fragrant, about 30 seconds. Add beans, remaining ¼ tsp salt, and remaining ⅛ tsp pepper and cook, stirring occasionally, until heated through, about 3 minutes.

4 Spoon beans into a large shallow serving bowl or plate and top with tomatoes and any accumulated juices from baking sheet. Sprinkle with basil.

Per serving (½ cup beans and about ½ cup tomatoes): 210 Cal, 4 g Total Fat, 1 g Sat Fat, 376 mg Sod, 34 g Total Carb, 4 g Sugar, 8 g Fib, 11 g Prot.

Spicy bulgur with carrots and harissa

Serves 4

2 **cups water**
1 **cup quick-cooking bulgur**
½ **tsp salt**
¼ **tsp black pepper**
1 **cup shredded or matchstick-cut carrots**
1 **cup frozen baby peas, thawed**
¾ **tsp harissa**
½ **cup chopped cilantro**

1 Combine water, bulgur, salt, and pepper in a large saucepan and bring to a boil. Reduce heat and simmer, covered, until bulgur is tender and water is absorbed, about 10 minutes.

2 Add carrots, peas, and harissa to bulgur and cook, stirring, until carrots are just tender, about 2 minutes. Stir in cilantro.

Per serving (1 cup): 160 Cal, 1 g Total Fat, 0 g Sat Fat, 362 mg Sod, 34 g Total Carb, 3 g Sugar, 7 g Fib, 6 g Prot.

Spicy bulgur with
carrots and harissa

Whole-grain tips and tricks

A grain is a whole grain when it has all three of its parts: the outer bran layer, which contains antioxidants, vitamins, and fiber; the endosperm, the largest portion of the grain kernel that contains starchy carbohydrates, proteins, and small amounts of vitamins and minerals; and the germ, which is the "heart" of the grain and from where a new plant can sprout.

When shopping, one of the easiest ways to spot a whole grain is to look for the whole-grain stamp on the package. The yellow and black stamp features a sheath of wheat and the words 100% Whole Grain. There is also a stamp for products where at least 50% of the product is whole grain and a stamp labeled Whole Grain for products that contain less than 50% whole grain.

Another way to know if you are buying a product that is 100% whole grain is to look for these key words:

- whole grain
- whole wheat
- whole (plus name of grain)
- stoneground whole (plus name of grain)
- brown rice
- oats
- old-fashioned, rolled, quick-cook, instant oatmeal
- wheat berries

Tip: A great shortcut is to cook up a double or triple batch of grain and refrigerate in a covered container for up to 4 days. Warm the grain up a bit by letting it sit on the counter or by heating it in the microwave or in a saucepan over low heat with a bit of water added.

Tip: Short on time? Look for shelf-stable precooked brown rice in supermarkets or frozen parcooked farro in the freezer section of big box stores.

Tip: The time it takes whole grains to cook depends on three things: the freshness of the grain, the type of grain, and the pot it's cooked in.

Trick: Presoaking some grains in a specified amount of cold water for several hours or up to overnight will significantly reduce the cooking time. After soaking, add a bit more water if needed and cook the grain until tender. The cooking time will depend on the type of grain and how long it was soaked.

Trick: Add more flavor to a grain by first cooking chopped onion or a combination of onion and minced garlic in a little oil. Then add the grain and cook, stirring, until softened before adding the water—or use broth or a combination of broth and water for more flavor.

Trick: If a grain begins to stick to the bottom of the pot during cooking, take the pot off the heat and add a little water. Cover and let stand for about 5 minutes, then stir the grain from the bottom of the pot using a wooden spoon or silicone spatula.

Cooking whole grains

Method: Put the grain into a pot with the specified amount of water and bring to a boil. Reduce the heat and simmer, covered, until the grain is tender, adding a bit more liquid if needed or pouring off any excess liquid.

To 1 cup of grain	Amount of liquid	Approximate cooking time	Approximate yield
Amaranth	2 cups	25 minutes	3½ cups
Barley, pearl	3 cups	50 minutes	3½ cups
Buckwheat (kasha)	2 cups	20 minutes	4 cups
Bulgur	2 cups	10 minutes soaking time	3 cups
Couscous, whole-wheat	2 cups	10 minutes soaking time	4 cups
Kamut	2½ cups	1½ hours	2½ cups
Millet	2½ cups	30 minutes	4 cups
Oats, steel-cut	4 cups	20 minutes	4 cups
Quinoa	2 cups	12 minutes	3 cups
Rice, brown (long grain)	2½ cups	30 minutes	3 cups
Rice, brown basmati	2 cups	45 minutes	4 cups
Rice, brown jasmine	2 cups	45 minutes	4 cups
Sorghum	4 cups	30 minutes	3 cups
Spelt	4 cups	soak overnight; cook 50 minutes	3 cups
Teff	3 cups	15 minutes	3 cups
Wheat berries	4 cups	soak overnight; cook 50 minutes	3 cups
Wild rice, cultivated	2½ cups	1 hour	4 cups
Wild rice, native	2½ cups	50 minutes	4 cups

Couscous with chickpeas and oranges

Serves 4

In just a few minutes, you can whip up your own seasoned rice vinegar. In a cup, mix together 1 tbsp rice vinegar, ¾ tsp superfine sugar, 1 tsp mirin or sake, and a pinch of salt until the sugar has dissolved.

Olive-oil nonstick spray

1¼ cups water

1 cup canned chickpeas, rinsed and drained

¼ tsp salt (or to taste)

⅛ tsp black pepper

1 cup whole-wheat couscous

2 large navel oranges

1 tbsp seasoned rice vinegar

¼ cup thinly sliced mint

1 Combine water, chickpeas, salt, and pepper in a medium saucepan and bring to a boil. Add couscous and remove saucepan from heat. Let stand, covered, until couscous is tender and water is absorbed, about 5 minutes.

2 Meanwhile, with sharp knife, peel oranges and remove white pith. Cut oranges into rounds and cut each round in quarters. Transfer couscous mixture to a serving bowl; add vinegar and lightly spray with nonstick spray, tossing until coated evenly. Add oranges and mint and gently toss until combined. Serve hot, warm, or at room temperature.

Per serving (1¼ cups): 294 Cal, 3 g Total Fat, 0 g Sat Fat, 308 mg Sod, 59 g Total Carb, 14 g Sugar, 12 g Fib, 12 g Prot.

Add this
Stir ½ tsp ground cumin into the couscous mixture along with the oranges and mint.

Mashed parsnips, potatoes, and apple

Serves 6

Browned butter is special. It has a nutty flavor that can turn almost any dish from ordinary into extraordinary. Stirred into mashed parsnips, potatoes, and apple that are seasoned with salt, pepper, and fresh thyme, it becomes a delectable side.

1   lb parsnips, peeled
    and cut into ½-inch slices

1   lb Yukon Gold
    potatoes, peeled and
    cut into ¾-inch chunks

1   large McIntosh apple,
    peeled, cored, and cut
    into ¾-inch chunks

1   cup water

2   tbsp unsalted
    butter

½   tsp chopped
    thyme

1   tsp salt

⅛   tsp black pepper

1 Combine parsnips, potatoes, apple, and water in a large saucepan and set over medium heat. Cook, covered, stirring occasionally, until vegetables have softened, about 20 minutes.

2 Meanwhile, melt butter in a small nonstick skillet over medium heat and cook until butter starts to foam. Swirl pan and cook until foam subsides and milk solids turn brown. Pour over parsnip mixture.

3 With a potato masher, mash parsnip mixture until it forms coarse puree. Stir in thyme, salt, and pepper. Stir in a bit of water if mixture seems dry, reheating over low heat if needed before serving.

Per serving (about ¾ cup): 161 Cal, 4 g Total Fat, 3 g Sat Fat, 409 mg Sod, 30 g Total Carb, 8 g Sugar, 6 g Fib, 2 g Prot.

Crispy
Hasselback
potatoes

Crispy Hasselback potatoes

Serves 4

This company-perfect potato dish is named after Stockholm's historic Hasselbacken Hotel, but it is also known as accordion potatoes in the U.S.

4   **(5-oz) Yukon Gold potatoes, scrubbed**

2   **tsp olive oil**

1   **large garlic clove, minced**

½   **tsp salt**

¼   **tsp black pepper**

Maldon sea salt (optional)

1 Preheat oven to 425°F. Line a small rimmed baking sheet with a sheet of parchment paper.

2 Peel potatoes, leaving lengthwise strip of skin on one long side of each potato. Place potatoes, skin-side down, on cutting board. With thin sharp knife, cut each potato crosswise into ⅛-inch slices, stopping about ¼ inch from bottom.

3 Drizzle potatoes with oil, gently separating slices so oil can seep down and coat potatoes. Sprinkle with garlic, salt, and pepper, separating slices to ensure seasoning coats every slice.

4 Place potatoes, skin-side down, on prepared baking sheet and bake until potatoes are browned and tender, about 50 minutes. Sprinkle with Maldon salt, if using.

Per serving (1 potato): 119 Cal, 2 g Total Fat, 0 g Sat Fat, 313 mg Sod, 22 g Total Carb, 2 g Sugar, 3 g Fib, 2 g Prot.

Add this
Add some finely minced thyme to the potatoes along with garlic.

Cast-iron skillet potato kugel

Serves 8

Gluten-free potato starch helps make this kugel (aka pudding) extra light. Potato starch is not the same as potato flour. Potato starch is made from the starch of the potato and is flavorless, while potato flour is made from the flesh.

Olive oil nonstick spray

1	**onion, cut into chunks**
2	**lb small russet potatoes, peeled**
2	**large eggs, lightly beaten**
¼	**cup potato starch**
1½	**tsp kosher salt**
¼	**tsp black pepper**
2	**tbsp olive oil**

1 Preheat oven to 350°F.

2 Finely chop onion in a food processor. Transfer to a large bowl. To create long shreds, trim potatoes so they fit horizontally in feed tube. With shredding blade in place, shred potatoes and add to onion. Add eggs, potato starch, salt, and pepper and stir until mixed well.

3 In a 10-inch cast-iron or other heavy ovenproof skillet over medium-high heat, warm oil until very hot. Add potato mixture (it should sizzle) in an even layer, twisting potato shreds on top to form decorative pattern. Spray with nonstick spray.

4 Bake until potatoes are golden and crisp on top and tender when knife is inserted, about 1 hour 10 minutes.

5 Cut kugel into 8 wedges and sprinkle with additional salt and pepper if desired.

Per serving (1 wedge): 163 Cal, 5 g Total Fat, 1 g Sat Fat, 386 mg Sod, 27 g Total Carb, 1 g Sugar, 2 g Fib, 4 g Prot.

Try this
The combination of potatoes and herbs are a perfect marriage. Add 2 tsp of chopped thyme or rosemary to the potatoes along with the eggs in step 2.

Cheddar potato "fries"

Serves 4

Crisp on the outside and oh-so-tender on the inside are the hallmarks of great fries. To ensure those qualities, keep the potatoes separated on the baking sheet so the heat of the oven touches every inch of the potatoes.

Nonstick spray

2 **(9-oz) russet potatoes**

¼ **tsp salt**

¼ **tsp black pepper**

½ **cup shredded reduced-fat cheddar**

1 Preheat oven to 400°F. Line a large rimmed baking sheet with silicone baking mat or sheet of parchment paper.

2 Peel potatoes and cut into ¼-inch-thick matchstick strips (you should have about 52 total). Put on prepared baking sheet. Spray potatoes with nonstick spray and sprinkle with salt and pepper, tossing to coat evenly. Spread potatoes to form an even layer, making sure they do not overlap or touch.

3 Bake potatoes 20 minutes. Turn fries over and spread out. Bake until golden brown, about 20 minutes longer. Gather fries together and sprinkle with cheddar. Bake until cheese has melted, about 5 minutes longer. Transfer fries with baking sheet to wire rack and let cool slightly before serving.

Per serving (about 13 "fries"): 142 Cal, 3 g Total Fat, 2 g Sat Fat, 240 mg Sod, 23 g Total Carb, 1 g Sugar, 3 g Fib, 6 g Prot.

German-style potato-sauerkraut salad

Serves 6

Potato salad, known as *kartoffelsalat* in Germany, is usually served warm. It sometimes contains bold-flavored mustard to give it a little punch, which would be a great addition to our salad.

8	small red potatoes, scrubbed
1	(¼-lb) piece skinless smoked turkey breast, cut into ½-inch dice
2	scallions, thinly sliced
1	tbsp extra-virgin olive oil
1	to 1½ tsp caraway seeds, crushed (optional)
½	tsp salt
¼	tsp black pepper
12	oz fresh sauerkraut (bagged or jarred), undrained (about 2 cups), at room temperature

1 Combine potatoes with enough salted water to cover by 1 inch in a small saucepan and bring to a boil. Reduce heat and simmer until potatoes are fork-tender, about 12 minutes. Drain and let cool about 5 minutes. Cut warm potatoes in quarters.

2 Combine potatoes, turkey, scallions, oil, caraway seeds (if using), salt, and pepper in a serving bowl. Add sauerkraut and gently toss until combined.

Per serving (⅔ cup): 213 Cal, 3 g Total Fat, 1 g Sat Fat, 700 mg Sod, 40 g Total Carb, 4 g Sugar, 6 g Fib, 8 g Prot.

German-style
potato-sauerkraut salad

**Smashed potatoes
with lemon salt**

Smashed potatoes with lemon salt

Serves 4

You can also make this delicious potato dish with smaller potatoes. Use 8 (2-oz) potatoes, and keep in mind that the cooking time will be reduced to about 12 minutes.

4	(¼-lb) red or yellow potatoes, scrubbed
¾	tsp kosher or coarse sea salt
½	tsp grated lemon zest
2	tsp extra-virgin olive oil
1	large garlic clove, thinly sliced
1	tbsp chopped parsley

1 Combine potatoes with enough salted water to cover by 1 inch in a medium saucepan and bring to boil. Reduce heat and simmer, covered, until potatoes are fork-tender, about 25 minutes. Drain potatoes and let cool about 5 minutes.

2 Meanwhile combine salt and lemon zest in a cup, rubbing them together with fingers to bring out lemon oil. Set aside.

3 Put potatoes on a cutting board and gently press down on each potato with palm of hand or a pancake spatula to flatten slightly (the edges of potatoes will split).

4 Combine oil and garlic in a large nonstick skillet and set over medium heat. Cook, stirring, until garlic is lightly toasted, about 1 minute. With a slotted spoon, lift out garlic and transfer to a separate cup.

5 Add potatoes to skillet and cook over medium-high heat until browned and crisp on bottom, about 5 minutes. With a small spatula, gently turn potatoes over and cook until second side is browned and crisp, about 5 minutes longer. Transfer potatoes to small platter and sprinkle with lemon salt, garlic chips, and parsley.

Per serving (1 potato): 101 Cal, 2 g Total Fat, 0 g Sat Fat, 383 mg Sod, 18 g Total Carb, 1 g Sugar, 2 g Fib, 2 g Prot.

Classic French potato salad

Serves 6

It's pure genius tossing still-warm cooked potatoes with a liquid such as stock or vinegar. This technique makes it easy for the potatoes to absorb it, flavoring them all the way through.

6   (¼-lb) Yukon Gold potatoes, peeled

2   tbsp champagne vinegar

⅓   to ½ cup chopped herbs, such as parsley, dill, and basil

2   scallions, finely chopped

1   large shallot, finely chopped (⅓ cup)

2   tbsp extra-virgin olive oil

¾   tsp salt

¼   tsp black pepper (or to taste)

1 Combine potatoes with enough salted water to cover by 1 inch in a medium saucepan and bring to a boil. Reduce heat and simmer, covered, until potatoes are tender, about 20 minutes. Drain and let cool about 5 minutes. Cut potatoes into ¾-inch chunks and transfer to a serving bowl.

2 Sprinkle vinegar over warm potatoes and gently toss to coat. Let stand 5 minutes, tossing once or twice. Add herbs, scallions, shallot, oil, salt, and pepper and gently toss until mixed well. Let stand, about 10 minutes. Serve warm or at room temperature.

Per serving (generous ¾ cup): 128 Cal, 5 g Total Fat, 1 g Sat Fat, 312 mg Sod, 20 g Total Carb, 2 g Sugar, 3 g Fib, 2 g Prot.

**Classic French
potato salad**

Savory spinach-Parmesan oats

Serves 4

On-trend and super-satisfying is the best way to describe this breakfast dish. Since it takes less than 20 minutes to prepare, it can likely fit into your weekday breakfast routine.

Nonstick spray

2   **scallions, thinly sliced**

3½ **cups water**

2   **cups old-fashioned (rolled) oats**

½   **tsp salt**

2   **cups lightly packed baby spinach**

¼   **tsp black pepper**

¼   **cup grated Parmesan**

2   **tsp extra-virgin olive oil**

1 Spray an 8-cup glass measure or microwavable bowl with nonstick spray. Add scallions and microwave on High until softened, about 1 minute.

2 Add water, oats, and salt to scallions. Cover with a piece of microwavable plastic wrap with one side folded back to vent or with microwavable plate. Microwave on High until oats have thickened, about 8 minutes, stirring about every minute.

3 Stir spinach and pepper into oat mixture. Let stand, covered, until spinach has wilted, about 1 minute. Spoon evenly into 4 bowls; sprinkle with Parmesan and drizzle with oil.

Per serving (1 cup oatmeal, 1 tbsp Parmesan, and ½ tsp olive oil): 213 Cal, 7 g Total Fat, 2 g Sat Fat, 423 mg Sod, 29 g Total Carb, 1 g Sugar, 5 g Fib, 9 g Prot.

Red quinoa with parsley and pine nuts

Serves 6

Quinoa has risen to star power. High in protein and fiber, it has a nutty flavor and invitingly chewy texture. Because its natural outer coating has a bitter flavor, always rinse quinoa unless it says "prerinsed" on the package.

2	cups water
1	cup red quinoa
½	tsp salt (or to taste)
1½	tbsp white wine vinegar
2	tsp extra-virgin olive oil
¼	tsp black pepper
⅓	cup chopped flat-leaf parsley
3	tbsp pine nuts, toasted

1 Bring water to a boil in a small saucepan; stir in quinoa and salt. Reduce heat and simmer, covered, until water is absorbed and quinoa is tender, about 15 minutes. Remove saucepan from heat and let stand 5 minutes; fluff quinoa with fork.

2 In a serving bowl, whisk together vinegar, oil, and pepper. Add quinoa, parsley, and pine nuts and toss until mixed well. Taste and season with additional salt, if desired.

Per serving (generous ½ cup): 144 Cal, 5 g Total Fat, 1 g Sat Fat, 200 mg Sod, 19 g Total Carb, 0 g Sugar, 2 g Fib, 5 g Prot.

**Polenta with
spinach and cheese**

Polenta with spinach and cheese

Serves 4

Comfort in a bowl describes this dish. Quick-cooking polenta gets extra flavor by being whisked into chicken broth instead of water. If you happen to have homemade stock in your freezer, use it here. Get the most enjoyment by eating this with a spoon!

2	**cups reduced-sodium chicken broth**
½	**cup instant polenta**
4	**cups lightly packed baby spinach**
¼	**tsp salt**
¼	**tsp black pepper**
¼	**cup grated Parmesan**

1 Bring broth to a boil in a medium saucepan over medium-high heat. Whisk in polenta in thin, steady stream. Stir in spinach, salt, and pepper.

2 Reduce heat to medium-low and cook, stirring occasionally, until polenta has thickened, about 4 minutes. Remove saucepan from heat and stir in Parmesan. Serve immediately.

Per serving (½ cup): 111 Cal, 2 g Total Fat, 1 g Sat Fat, 559 mg Sod, 18 g Total Carb, 0 g Sugar, 2 g Fib, 6 g Prot.

The real deal fried rice

Serves 6

What makes this fried rice authentic is the omission of soy sauce, which is the typical way to serve it in China. That said, there is nothing wrong with serving soy sauce at the table.

1	**tsp canola or peanut oil**
1	**(6-oz) piece lean ham steak, diced**
4	**various color mini sweet peppers, diced (1 cup)**
5	**scallions, sliced (green and white parts separated)**
2	**(8½-oz) pouches ready-to-serve basmati rice**
¼	**cup water**
½	**tsp salt**
⅛	**tsp black pepper**
2	**large eggs, beaten**

1 In a large nonstick skillet over high heat, warm oil. Add ham, sweet peppers, and white part of scallions and cook, stirring occasionally, until peppers are tender and lightly colored in spots, about 6 minutes.

2 Add rice, water, salt, and black pepper and cook, breaking up rice and scraping bottom of skillet to lift up any browned bits, until rice is hot, about 3 minutes.

3 Push rice mixture to one side of skillet and pour beaten eggs into empty side of skillet. Cook until eggs begin to set on bottom, about 1 minute; stir eggs and cook until set, breaking them up, 2 minutes longer. Stir eggs and green part of scallions into rice mixture.

Per serving (⅔ cup): 227 Cal, 7 g Total Fat, 1 g Sat Fat, 673 mg Sod, 30 g Total Carb, 1 g Sugar, 3 g Fib, 11 g Prot.

**The real deal
fried rice**

Coconut-cardamom basmati rice

Serves 6

1   **cup water**
1   **cup brown basmati rice**
1   **cup light (low-fat) coconut milk**
½   **tsp ground cardamom**
½   **tsp salt**
⅛   **tsp black pepper**

Bring water to a boil in a medium saucepan. Add rice, coconut milk, cardamom, salt, and pepper and return to a boil. Reduce heat and simmer, covered, until rice is tender and liquid is absorbed, about 40 minutes.

Per serving (½ cup): 141 Cal, 3 g Total Fat, 2 g Sat Fat, 197 mg Sod, 26 g Total Carb, 0 g Sugar, 0 g Fib, 2 g Prot.

Serving idea
This side dish, fragrant from basmati rice and richly flavored from coconut milk, would pair well with broiled or grilled salt and pepper seasoned shrimp.

Roasted garlic–herb bread

Serves 6

Our irresistible roasted garlic-Parmesan mixture is also great spooned over steamed green beans, spread over grilled chicken or salmon steaks, or used as a topping for steamed baby potatoes.

Olive-oil nonstick spray

1   **head garlic**

¼   **cup grated Parmesan**

¾   **tsp dried Italian seasoning**

½   **(12-oz) whole-grain or whole-wheat baguette, sliced lengthwise in half**

1 Preheat oven to 375°F.

2 Cut head of garlic crosswise in half. Lightly spray all over with nonstick spray and tightly wrap in a sheet of foil. Place foil package directly on oven rack and roast until garlic is very tender when squeezed, about 1 hour.

3 When cool enough to handle, unwrap garlic and squeeze out pulp from each clove into a small bowl. Add Parmesan and Italian seasoning, mashing mixture with fork until smooth and combined.

4 Preheat broiler.

5 Spread garlic-Parmesan mixture over cut sides of bread. Place bread, cut-side up, on broiler rack and broil 5 inches from heat until browned in spots and heated through, about 2 minutes. Cut bread into 12 pieces.

Per serving (2 pieces): 107 Cal, 2 g Total Fat, 1 g Sat Fat, 208 mg Sod, 17 g Total Carb, 1 g Sugar, 2 g Fib, 6 g Prot.

Mixed rice pilaf with orange

Serves 6

1	**tbsp olive oil**
1	**small onion, chopped**
1	**celery stalk, cut into small dice**
1½	**cups water**
	Grated zest and juice of 1 orange
½	**tsp salt**
¼	**tsp black pepper**
1	**cup brown and wild rice blend**
¼	**cup dried currants**

1 In a medium saucepan over medium heat, warm oil. Add onion and celery and cook, stirring, until softened, about 5 minutes. Add water, ¼ cup of orange juice (save remaining juice for another use), salt, and pepper and bring to boil. Stir in rice. Reduce heat and simmer, covered, until rice is tender and liquid is absorbed, about 45 minutes, sprinkling currants on top during last 5 minutes of cooking.

2 Remove saucepan from heat and let stand, covered, 10 minutes. Fluff rice with fork and stir in orange zest. Transfer to serving bowl.

Per serving (about ⅔ cup): 88 Cal, 3 g Total Fat, 0 g Sat Fat, 312 mg Sod, 15 g Total Carb, 7 g Sugar, 2 g Fib, 2 g Prot.

**Mixed rice pilaf
with orange**

Chapter 7
Sweet nothings

Plum crostata, 187

Baked almond crisp–topped peaches, 188

Chocolate-orange mousse, 189

Red wine–poached pears, 190

Matcha-chocolate meringue bark, 192

Banana–chocolate chip "ice cream," 193

Vanilla-bean panna cotta, 195

Hibiscus granita with grilled mango, 197

Plum crostata

Plum crostata

Serves 8

Nonstick spray

4 **large plums (about 1½ lb), halved, pitted, and cut into thin wedges**

⅓ **cup plus 1 tbsp sugar, divided**

1½ **tbsp all-purpose flour**

¼ **tsp ground cinnamon or ⅛ tsp freshly grated nutmeg**

1 **refrigerated piecrust (from 14.1-oz package), softened according to package directions**

1 Preheat oven to 400°F. Line a large baking sheet with a sheet of heavy foil or parchment paper; lightly spray with nonstick spray.

2 To make filling: In a medium bowl, toss together plums, ⅓ cup sugar, flour, and cinnamon.

3 On a lightly floured work surface with a floured rolling pin, roll piecrust into 13-inch round. Fold piecrust in quarters; transfer to prepared baking sheet and gently unfold, being careful not to stretch dough.

4 Pile plum mixture on piecrust, leaving 1½- to 2-inch border. Scatter any sugar mixture remaining in bowl over plums. Fold edge of piecrust over filling, pleating it as you go. Sprinkle remaining 1 tbsp sugar over plums. Bake until filling is bubbly and crust is golden, about 45 minutes. Let cool on baking sheet on wire rack.

Per serving (⅛ of crostata): 210 Cal, 8 g Total Fat, 3 g Sat Fat, 117 mg Sod, 36 g Total Carb, 19 g Sugar, 2 g Fib, 2 g Prot.

Baked almond crisp–topped peaches

Serves 8

An old-fashioned crisp is a simple country-style dessert where fruit is topped with a mix of flour, brown sugar, and butter and baked. We used halved peaches because it's even easier to coat them with our topping, which includes almonds and oats for crunch.

Nonstick spray

4   **(6-oz) firm-ripe peaches, halved and pitted**

¼   **cup whole almonds**

¼   **cup packed light brown sugar**

⅛   **tsp salt**

2   **tbsp cold unsalted butter, cut into pieces**

⅓   **cup old-fashioned (rolled) oats**

1 Preheat oven to 375°F.

2 Place peaches, cut-side up, in a small shallow baking dish that has been sprayed with nonstick spray. Combine almonds, brown sugar, and salt in a food processor and pulse until almonds are coarsely chopped. Add butter and pulse until mixture is evenly moistened and forms small clumps; add oats and pulse until just mixed. Spoon about 3 tbsp of almond mixture into center of each peach, pressing lightly to cover peaches.

3 Bake until topping is golden brown and crisp, and peaches are tender when pierced with knife but still hold their shape, about 40 minutes. Transfer peaches to wire rack and let cool about 10 minutes. Serve warm or at room temperature.

Per serving (½ stuffed peach): 115 Cal, 5 g Total Fat, 2 g Sat Fat, 75 mg Sod, 18 g Total Carb, 14 g Sugar, 2 g Fib, 2 g Prot.

Chocolate-orange mousse

Serves 8

If you accidentally over-whisk the chocolate mixture and it turns grainy, simply re-melt it over very low heat and whisk again.

2   **small oranges**
½   **cup refrigerated liquid egg whites**
¼   **cup confectioners' sugar**
⅔   **cup bittersweet chocolate chips**
⅓   **cup boiling water**
Ice water
1   **(6-oz) container orange crème low-fat whipped or custard-style yogurt**

1 Grate ½ tsp zest from 1 orange; reserve. Section both oranges and cut sections crosswise in half; refrigerate if leaving out for more than 2 hours.

2 With electric mixer on low speed, beat egg whites and confectioners' sugar in a large bowl until sugar has dissolved. Increase speed to medium-high and beat until stiff peaks form when beaters are lifted, about 10 minutes, scraping down side of bowl once or twice.

3 Put chocolate chips in a medium bowl and pour boiling water over. Wait about 30 seconds, then stir until chocolate is melted and mixture is smooth. Place bowl of chocolate over larger bowl filled with ice water. Whisk constantly, until chocolate is just thickened to consistency of soft pudding, 2 to 3 minutes.

4 Immediately remove whipped chocolate from ice water and gently fold in yogurt, orange zest, and large spoonful of beaten whites to lighten mixture. Fold in remaining whites just until no longer visible. Spoon mousse into 8 dessert glasses, dividing evenly. Refrigerate until set, about 2 hours or up to 6 hours.

5 To serve, top each serving of mousse with orange sections.

Per serving (½ cup mousse and about 3 orange sections): 149 Cal, 6 g Total Fat, 4 g Sat Fat, 40 mg Sod, 22 g Total Carb, 18 g Sugar, 2 g Fib, 4 g Prot.

Red wine–poached pears

Serves 6

Wine-poached pears are as classic and elegant as a simple black dress that never goes out of style. In this recipe, the pears are poached in a flavorful red-wine mixture until tender enough to be easily pierced with a paring knife.

1½ **cups dry red wine, such as merlot or Cabernet Sauvignon**

1 **cup water**

¼ **cup sugar**

2 **(3-inch) strips lemon zest, removed with vegetable peeler**

1 **(3-inch) cinnamon stick**

6 **(5-oz) firm-ripe Bartlett or Bosc pears with stems**

1 Combine wine, water, sugar, lemon zest, and cinnamon stick in a saucepan just large enough to hold pears and set over medium heat. Cook, stirring occasionally, until sugar has dissolved. Remove saucepan from heat.

2 Meanwhile, peel pears leaving stems intact. Add pears to wine mixture and bring to a boil. Reduce heat to low and simmer, covered, turning pears occasionally, until pears are evenly colored and tender when pierced with knife, about 30 minutes.

3 With a slotted spoon, transfer pears to a large bowl. Pour poaching liquid through a fine sieve set over a medium saucepan and bring to a boil. Cook until syrupy and reduced to about ½ cup, about 20 minutes. Let cool to room temperature.

4 Transfer pears to a large zip-close plastic bag and add cooled syrup. Squeeze out most of air and seal bag. Gently turn bag to coat pears. Put bag with pears in a large bowl and refrigerate at least overnight or up to 4 days, turning bag several times.

5 To serve, place pears on dessert plates and spoon syrup over.

Per serving (1 pear and about 1 tbsp syrup): 195 Cal, 0 g Total Fat, 0 g Sat Fat, 5 mg Sod, 37 g Total Carb, 26 g Sugar, 6 g Fib, 1 g Prot.

Red wine–poached pears

Matcha-chocolate meringue bark

Serves 16

Don't be daunted by the idea of making a meringue. It's nothing more than egg whites beaten with sugar—your mixer does all the work. The only thing to keep in mind is that meringue should be made on a day when the humidity is low or it won't crisp.

1	**tbsp water**
2	**tsp matcha (green-tea powder)**
5	**large egg whites, at room temperature**
½	**cup superfine sugar**
2	**tbsp mini semisweet chocolate chips**
4	**tsp toasted sesame seeds**

1 Preheat oven to 250°F. Line a large rimmed baking sheet with a sheet of parchment paper.

2 Stir together water and matcha in a cup. With an electric mixer on medium speed, beat egg whites in a large bowl until soft peaks form when beaters are lifted. Beat in sugar, 1 tbsp at a time, until stiff, glossy peaks form. Beat in matcha mixture until meringue is pale green, about 1 minute longer.

3 Place a dab of meringue on the underside of each corner of parchment to help keep parchment in place. Pile meringue on parchment and spread with an offset spatula to form 9 x 12-inch rectangle (about ¾-inch thick). Sprinkle chocolate chips and sesame seeds evenly over meringue.

4 Bake until meringue looks dry and set but is slightly soft in center when gently pressed, about 2½ hours. Turn off oven and leave meringue in oven until meringue is firm and crisp, at least 4 hours or up to overnight. (Meringue will turn light beige.)

5 Turn meringue bark with parchment over and carefully peel off parchment. Turn meringue bark right-side up. Using serrated knife, gently cut into 16 pieces. The bark is best served on the day it is prepared.

Per serving (1 piece): 43 Cal, 1 g Total Fat, 0 g Sat Fat, 17 mg Sod, 8 g Total Carb, 7 g Sugar, 1 g Fib, 1 g Prot.

Banana-chocolate chip "ice cream"

Serves 4

4	ripe large bananas
½	tsp vanilla extract
¼	cup mini semisweet chocolate chips
2	tbsp sliced almonds, toasted

1 Peel bananas and cut into 1-inch chunks. Place in a large zip-close plastic bag. Squeeze out air and seal bag. Place in freezer until bananas are frozen solid, at least 3 hours or up to overnight.

2 Put frozen bananas in a food processor and puree, scraping down side of food processor with a rubber spatula once or twice. Add vanilla and pulse until mixed. Transfer to a medium bowl and stir in chocolate chips.

3 Scoop ice cream into 4 dessert dishes and sprinkle with almonds. Or cover and freeze up to 1 day, leaving ice cream out on counter about 10 minutes before serving for easier scooping.

Per serving (½ cup "ice cream" and 1½ tsp almonds): 191 Cal, 5 g Total Fat, 2 g Sat Fat, 2 mg Sod, 39 g Total Carb, 21 g Sugar, 5 g Fib, 3 g Prot.

**Vanilla-bean
panna cotta**

Vanilla-bean panna cotta

Serves 4

This tasty light Italian dessert is simply an eggless custard. Our recipe is easily doubled, making it perfect for dinner parties and occasions.

Nonstick spray

1¼ tsp unflavored gelatin

2 tbsp cold water

1 vanilla bean, split, or ¾ tsp vanilla extract

1 cup low-fat buttermilk

¾ cup half-and-half

¼ cup sugar

1 Lightly spray 4 (5-oz) ramekins, (6-oz) custard cups, or wineglasses with nonstick spray.

2 Sprinkle gelatin over water in a cup. Let stand until gelatin has softened, about 5 minutes.

3 Meanwhile, with edge of a small knife, split vanilla-bean pod and scrape out seeds, reserving both pod and seeds.

4 In a small saucepan over medium heat, combine buttermilk, half-and-half, sugar, and vanilla pod and seeds. Cook, whisking occasionally, until mixture is hot and sugar has dissolved, 4 to 5 minutes. Remove saucepan from heat and add gelatin mixture, whisking until it has completely dissolved. Pour panna cotta through a sieve set over a medium bowl or glass measure. Stir in vanilla extract, if using.

5 Divide custard mixture evenly among prepared ramekins. Refrigerate until panna cotta is chilled and set, at least 4 hours or up to 1 day.

Per serving (1 panna cotta): 133 Cal, 5 g Total Fat, 4 g Sat Fat, 145 mg Sod, 18 g Total Carb, 17 g Sugar, 0 g Fib, 4 g Prot.

Serving idea
Top each panna cotta with a few raspberries for a sweet-tart bite.

**Hibiscus granita
with grilled mango**

Hibiscus granita with grilled mango

Serves 4

Did you know that a baking pan is made of metal while a baking dish is glass or ceramic? We used a metal baking pan in this recipe because it speeds up the freezing process.

Nonstick spray

6 **hibiscus-berry tea bags**

1½ **cups boiling water**

1 **lime, halved**

1½ **cups ice water**

3 **tbsp light agave nectar**

2 **firm-ripe mangoes**

1 Place tea bags in a 1-quart glass measure. Add boiling water and steep 30 minutes.

2 Meanwhile, squeeze juice from half of lime and set aside; cut remaining half into 4 wedges.

3 Remove tea bags and squeeze out liquid; discard bags. Add ice water, lime juice, and agave nectar to tea, stirring until blended. Pour tea mixture into an 8-inch square baking pan. Cover pan with foil and freeze until mixture is frozen along edges but still slushy in center, about 2 hours. With a fork, scrape icy edges in toward center. Repeat every 30 minutes until granita is semifirm and granular.

4 Place mango on a cutting board and cut off a thick slice on one side of the pit. Repeat on other side. With the tip of a knife, lightly score flesh.

5 Meanwhile, set a ridged grill pan over medium heat until hot. Lightly spray cut sides of mango with nonstick spray. Place mango, cut-side down, in grill pan and cook, turning once, until mango is tender and nicely marked, about 4 minutes.

6 To serve, with a fork, scrape granita, transferring ice shards to 4 dessert dishes. Place mango and lime wedges alongside.

Per serving (about ⅔ cup granita and ½ mango): 152 Cal, 1 g Total Fat, 0 g Sat Fat, 5 mg Sod, 39 g Total Carb, 34 g Sugar, 4 g Fib, 2 g Prot.

Recipes by SmartPoints® value

Green

0 SmartPoints
South-of-the-border salad, 71
Whole roasted tandoori cauliflower, 131

1 SmartPoints
Braised red cabbage and pears, 125
Carrot–horseradish puree, 128
Cauliflower with lemon and cumin, 129
Cheesy kale crisps, 45
Chunky cucumber-yogurt salad, 72
Double orange–mint salad, 75
Greek tzatziki dip, 37
Grilled zucchini with feta and lemon, 147
Lemony fennel and radicchio, 137
Roasted acorn squash with thyme, 143
Root vegetable chips, 44
Rosemary-roasted radishes, 141
Stir-fried garlic spinach, 142
Tomato and garlic–stuffed peppers, 144
Very French grated carrot salad, 127

2 SmartPoints
Crab salad–topped cucumber, 36
Lemon and pecorino popcorn, 47
Lemon barley, 154
Matcha-chocolate meringue bark, 192
Parmesan-pepper green bean "fries," 43
Provençal tomato tart, 38
Quick-cook fresh tomato sauce, 146
Sesame broccoli, 124
Soba noodle–mushroom soup, 57
Thai egg drop soup, 61
Three-vegetable tian, 149

3 SmartPoints
Baked tilapia with grapes and olives, 85
Banana–chocolate chip "ice cream," 193
Cheddar potato "fries," 167
Chicken kebabs with pineapple, 97
Coconut-cucumber splash, 31
Coconut-cumin green beans, 135
Flounder in crazy water, 87
Green sauce–marinated shrimp, 91
Hibiscus granita with grilled mango, 197
Hot and smoky pink beans, 155
Lotsa fruit spritzers, 32
Marinated tofu and vegetable kebabs, 119
Miso soup with tofu and scallions, 53
Mixed rice pilaf with orange, 182

Mustardy deviled eggs, 33
Niçoise-inspired tuna salad, 67
Polenta with spinach and cheese, 177
Roasted Brussels sprouts with walnuts, 122
Roasted garlic–herb bread, 181
Romaine and sun-dried tomato salad, 70
Silky chickpea soup with cumin, 50
Simple potato-leek soup, 60
Smashed potatoes with lemon salt, 171

4 SmartPoints
Baked almond crisp–topped peaches, 188
Baked eggs in tomatoes Florentine, 8
Catfish with salsa and olives, 88
Cherry and thyme–stuffed pork, 110
Chicken with black bean sauce, 94
Chickpea-broccoli soup, 63
Chunky guacamole–topped rice cakes, 34
Classic French potato salad, 172
Crispy Hasselback potatoes, 165
Fresh corn-basil soup, 52
Fresh pea salad with bacon, 74
Gin-basil smash, 27
Greens with Gorgonzola and almonds, 65
Hearty turkey-barley stew, 102
Hoisin-marinated London broil, 103
Mango-coconut agua fresca, 29
Miso-glazed salmon, 84
Pea soup with smoked salmon, 59
Peas with crispy prosciutto, 139
Red quinoa with parsley and pine nuts, 175
Red wine–poached pears, 190
Roast beef and Napa cabbage slaw, 64
Skinny breakfast sausages and eggs, 12
Spicy blue cheese–chicken burgers, 95
Spicy bulgur with carrots and harissa, 158
Sumac-dusted onion and chickpeas, 78
Warm roasted butternut squash salad, 68

5 SmartPoints
Bacon and cheddar–coddled eggs, 13
Broccoli-egg strudel, 5
Cast-iron skillet potato kugel, 166
Chilaquiles bake, 16
Coconut-cardamom basmati rice, 180
Coconut-curry tomato soup, 62
Curried barley with apricots, 152
Gruyère and asparagus frittata, 3
Mashed parsnips, potatoes, and apple, 163
North African red lentil soup, 54
Polenta with brown-sugar ricotta, 21
Reuben-style quesadillas, 41
Savory steel-cut oats with kale, 17
Stir-fried tofu with scallions, 115

Tropical oats with chia seeds, 18
White beans with roasted tomatoes, 157

6 SmartPoints
Braised Italian-style pork chops, 108
Coffee and chili–crusted tenderloin, 107
"Creamed" corn, 134
German-style potato-sauerkraut salad, 168
Grilled Parmesan corn on the cob, 132
Grilled Swiss chard and tomato pizzas, 109
Grilled turkey saltimbocca, 101
Pan-glazed turkey tenderloin, 99
Red quinoa salad with oranges, 76
Red, white, and blue parfaits, 23
Savory spinach-Parmesan oats, 174
Seared scallops with edamame puree, 89
The real deal fried rice, 178
Watermelon mojitos, 28

7 SmartPoints
Chocolate-orange mousse, 189
Couscous with chickpeas and oranges, 162
Greek-style breakfast pitas, 11
Kielbasa and lentil stew, 104
Maple breakfast pudding, 20
Overstuffed Western omelette, 4
Pecan-crusted buttermilk chicken, 92
Plum crostata, 187
Polenta "pizza" margherita, 116
Vanilla-bean panna cotta, 195

8 SmartPoints
Butterflied lamb with couscous salad, 112
Cheddar grits with bacon and kale, 14
Edamame-tomato bruschetta, 40
Zucchini and goat cheese omelette, 7

9 SmartPoints
Fresh salmon-ginger burgers, 82

10 SmartPoints
Spaghettini with limas and tomatoes, 114

11 SmartPoints
Turkey fingers with peach sauce, 98

Blue

0 SmartPoints
Hot and smoky pink beans, 155
South-of-the-border salad, 71
Thai egg drop soup, 61
Whole roasted tandoori cauliflower, 131

1 SmartPoints
Braised red cabbage and pears, 125
Carrot-horseradish puree, 128

Cauliflower with lemon and cumin, 129
Cheesy kale crisps, 45
Chicken kebabs with pineapple, 97
Chilaquiles bake, 16
"Creamed" corn, 134
Double orange–mint salad, 75
Fresh corn-basil soup, 52
Greek tzatziki dip, 37
Grilled zucchini with feta and lemon, 147
Lemony fennel and radicchio, 137
Marinated tofu and vegetable kebabs, 119
Miso-glazed salmon, 84
Miso soup with tofu and scallions, 53
Mustardy deviled eggs, 33
North African red lentil soup, 54
Quick-cook fresh tomato sauce, 146
Roasted acorn squash with thyme, 143
Root vegetable chips, 44
Rosemary-roasted radishes, 141
Seared scallops with edamame puree, 89
Stir-fried garlic spinach, 142
Sumac-dusted onion and chickpeas, 78
Stir-fried garlic spinach, 142
Tomato and garlic–stuffed peppers, 144
Very French grated carrot salad, 127
White beans with roasted tomatoes, 157

2 SmartPoints
Baked eggs in tomatoes Florentine, 8
Baked tilapia with grapes and olives, 85
Catfish with salsa and olives, 88
Chickpea-broccoli soup, 63
Chunky cucumber-yogurt salad, 72
Crab salad–topped cucumber, 36
Flounder in crazy water, 87
Green sauce–marinated shrimp, 91
Grilled Parmesan corn on the cob, 132
Lemon and pecorino popcorn, 47
Lemon barley, 154
Matcha-chocolate meringue bark, 192
Parmesan-pepper green bean "fries," 43
Pea soup with smoked salmon, 59
Peas with crispy prosciutto, 139
Provençal tomato tart, 38
Quick-cook fresh tomato sauce, 146
Sesame broccoli, 124
Skinny breakfast sausages and eggs, 12
Spicy blue cheese–chicken burgers, 95
Soba noodle–mushroom soup, 57
Three-vegetable tian, 149

3 SmartPoints
Bacon and cheddar–coddled eggs, 13
Banana–chocolate chip "ice cream," 193
Cheddar potato "fries," 167
Chicken with black bean sauce, 94
Coconut-cucumber splash, 31

Coconut-cumin green beans, 135
Fresh pea salad with bacon, 74
Fresh salmon-ginger burgers, 82
Gruyère and asparagus frittata, 3
Hearty turkey-barley stew, 102
Hibiscus granita with grilled mango, 197
Lotsa fruit spritzers, 32
Mixed rice pilaf with orange, 182
Niçoise-inspired tuna salad, 67
Overstuffed Western omelette, 4
Polenta with spinach and cheese, 177
Roasted Brussels sprouts with walnuts, 122
Roasted garlic–herb bread, 181
Romaine and sun-dried tomato salad, 70
Silky chickpea soup with cumin, 50
Simple potato-leek soup, 60
Smashed potatoes with lemon salt, 171
Spicy bulgur with carrots and harissa, 158
Stir-fried tofu with scallions, 115

4 SmartPoints
Baked almond crisp–topped peaches, 188
Broccoli-egg strudel, 5
Cast-iron skillet potato kugel, 166
Cherry and thyme–stuffed pork, 110
Chunky guacamole–topped rice cakes, 34
Classic French potato salad, 172
Crispy Hasselback potatoes, 165
Gin-basil smash, 27
Greek-style breakfast pitas, 11
Greens with Gorgonzola and almonds, 65
Grilled turkey saltimbocca, 101
Hoisin-marinated London broil, 103
Mango-coconut agua fresca, 29
Pan-glazed turkey tenderloin, 99
Pecan-crusted buttermilk chicken, 92
Red quinoa with parsley and pine nuts, 175
Red wine–poached pears, 190
Reuben-style quesadillas, 41
Roast beef and Napa cabbage slaw, 64
Warm roasted butternut squash salad, 68

5 SmartPoints
Coconut-cardamom basmati rice, 180
Coconut-curry tomato soup, 62
Couscous with chickpeas and oranges, 162
Curried barley with apricots, 152
Kielbasa and lentil stew, 104
Mashed parsnips, potatoes, and apple, 163
Polenta with brown-sugar ricotta, 21
Savory steel-cut oats with kale, 17
The real deal fried rice, 178
Tropical oats with chia seeds, 18

6 SmartPoints
Braised Italian-style pork chops, 108
Coffee and chili–crusted tenderloin, 107

Edamame-tomato bruschetta, 40
German-style potato-sauerkraut salad, 168
Grilled Swiss chard and tomato pizzas, 109
Red quinoa salad with oranges, 76
Red, white, and blue parfaits, 23
Savory spinach-Parmesan oats, 174
Watermelon mojitos, 28
Zucchini and goat cheese omelette, 7

7 SmartPoints
Chocolate-orange mousse, 189
Maple breakfast pudding, 20
Plum crostata, 187
Polenta "pizza" margherita, 116
Spaghettini with limas and tomatoes, 114
Vanilla-bean panna cotta, 195

8 SmartPoints
Butterflied lamb with couscous salad, 112
Cheddar grits with bacon and kale, 14

10 SmartPoints
Turkey fingers with peach sauce, 98

Purple

0 SmartPoints
Couscous with chickpeas and oranges, 162
Hot and smoky pink beans, 155
Pea soup with smoked salmon, 59
Root vegetable chips, 44
Simple potato-leek soup, 60
Soba noodle–mushroom soup, 57
South-of-the-border salad, 71
Spicy bulgur with carrots and harissa, 158
Thai egg drop soup, 61
Whole roasted tandoori cauliflower, 131

1 SmartPoints
Braised red cabbage and pears, 125
Carrot-horseradish puree, 128
Cauliflower with lemon and cumin, 129
Cheddar potato "fries," 167
Cheesy kale crisps, 45
Chicken kebabs with pineapple, 97
Chilaquiles bake, 16
Classic French potato salad, 172
"Creamed" corn, 134
Crispy Hasselback potatoes, 165
Double orange–mint salad, 75
Fresh corn-basil soup, 52
German-style potato-sauerkraut salad, 168
Greek tzatziki dip, 37
Grilled zucchini with feta and lemon, 147
Hearty turkey-barley stew, 102

Lemon and pecorino popcorn, 47
Lemon barley, 154
Lemony fennel and radicchio, 137
Marinated tofu and vegetable kebabs, 119
Miso-glazed salmon, 84
Miso soup with tofu and scallions, 53
Mustardy deviled eggs, 33
Niçoise-inspired tuna salad, 67
North African red lentil soup, 54
Red quinoa with parsley and pine nuts, 175
Roasted acorn squash with thyme, 143
Rosemary-roasted radishes, 141
Savory steel-cut oats with kale, 17
Seared scallops with edamame puree, 89
Smashed potatoes with lemon salt, 171
Stir-fried garlic spinach, 142
Sumac-dusted onion and chickpeas, 78
Tomato and garlic–stuffed peppers, 144
Very French grated carrot salad, 127
White beans with roasted tomatoes, 157

2 SmartPoints
Baked eggs in tomatoes Florentine, 8
Baked tilapia with grapes and olives, 85
Cast-iron skillet potato kugel, 166
Catfish with salsa and olives, 88
Chickpea-broccoli soup, 63
Chunky cucumber-yogurt salad, 72
Crab salad–topped cucumber, 36
Curried barley with apricots, 152
Flounder in crazy water, 87
Green sauce–marinated shrimp, 91
Grilled Parmesan corn on the cob, 132
Mashed parsnips, potatoes, and apple, 163
Matcha-chocolate meringue bark, 192
Parmesan-pepper green bean "fries," 43
Peas with crispy prosciutto, 139
Provençal tomato tart, 38
Quick-cook fresh tomato sauce, 146
Red quinoa salad with oranges, 76
Savory spinach-Parmesan oats, 174
Sesame broccoli, 124
Skinny breakfast sausages and eggs, 12
Spicy blue cheese–chicken burgers, 95
Three-vegetable tian, 149

3 SmartPoints
Bacon and cheddar–coddled eggs, 13
Baked almond crisp–topped peaches, 188
Banana–chocolate chip "ice cream," 193
Chicken with black bean sauce, 94
Coconut-cucumber splash, 31
Coconut-cumin green beans, 135
Fresh pea salad with bacon, 74
Fresh salmon-ginger burgers, 82
Gruyère and asparagus frittata, 3
Hibiscus granita with grilled mango, 197

Lotsa fruit spritzers, 32
Mixed rice pilaf with orange, 182
Overstuffed Western omelette, 4
Polenta with spinach and cheese, 177
Roasted Brussels sprouts with walnuts, 122
Roasted garlic–herb bread, 181
Romaine and sun-dried tomato salad, 70
Silky chickpea soup with cumin, 50
Stir-fried tofu with scallions, 115
Tropical oats with chia seeds, 18

4 SmartPoints
Broccoli-egg strudel, 5
Butterflied lamb with couscous salad, 112
Cherry and thyme–stuffed pork, 110
Chunky guacamole–topped rice cakes, 34
Gin-basil smash, 27
Greek-style breakfast pitas, 11
Greens with Gorgonzola and almonds, 65
Grilled turkey saltimbocca, 101
Hoisin-marinated London broil, 103
Mango-coconut agua fresca, 29
Maple breakfast pudding, 20
Pan-glazed turkey tenderloin, 99
Pecan-crusted buttermilk chicken, 92
Red wine–poached pears, 190
Reuben-style quesadillas, 41
Roast beef and Napa cabbage slaw, 64
Warm roasted butternut squash salad, 68

5 SmartPoints
Coconut-cardamom basmati rice, 180
Coconut-curry tomato soup, 62
Kielbasa and lentil stew, 104
Polenta with brown-sugar ricotta, 21
The real deal fried rice, 178

6 SmartPoints
Braised Italian-style pork chops, 108
Coffee and chili–crusted tenderloin, 107
Edamame-tomato bruschetta, 40
Grilled Swiss chard and tomato pizzas, 109
Red, white, and blue parfaits, 23
Watermelon mojitos, 28
Zucchini and goat cheese omelette, 7

7 SmartPoints
Chocolate-orange mousse, 189
Plum crostata, 187
Polenta "pizza" margherita, 116
Spaghettini with limas and tomatoes, 114
Vanilla-bean panna cotta, 195

8 SmartPoints
Cheddar grits with bacon and kale, 14

10 SmartPoints
Turkey fingers with peach sauce, 98

Index

A

Acorn squash
Roasted acorn squash with thyme, 143

Agave nectar
Coconut-cucumber splash, 31
Gin-basil smash, 27
Hibiscus granita with grilled mango, 197
Watermelon mojitos, 28

Alcohol, vii

Aleppo pepper, xiii

Almonds
Baked almond crisp-topped peaches, 188
Banana–chocolate chip "ice cream," 193
Greens with Gorgonzola and almonds, 65

Anchovies
Tomato and garlic–stuffed peppers, 144

Appetizers
Cheesy kale crisps, 45
Chunky guacamole-topped rice cakes, 34
Crab salad–topped cucumber, 36
Edamame-tomato bruschetta, 40
Greek tzatziki dip, 37
Lemon and pecorino popcorn, 47
Mustardy deviled eggs, 33
Parmesan-pepper green bean "fries," 43
Provençal tomato tart, 38
Reuben-style quesadillas, 41
Root vegetable chips, 44

Apples
Mashed parsnips, potatoes, and apple, 163

Apricots
Curried barley with apricots, 152

Arugula
Warm roasted butternut squash salad, 68

Asparagus
Chicken with black bean sauce, 94
Grilled turkey saltimbocca, 101
Gruyère and asparagus frittata, 3

Avocado
Chunky guacamole-topped rice cakes, 34

B

Bacon. *See also* Canadian bacon; turkey bacon
Bacon and cheddar–coddled eggs, 13
Fresh pea salad with bacon, 74
Roasted Brussels sprouts with walnuts, 122
Baked almond crisp-topped peaches, 188
Baked eggs in tomatoes Florentine, 8
Banana–chocolate chip "ice cream," 193

Barley
Curried barley with apricots, 152
Hearty turkey-barley stew, 102
Lemon barley, 154

Basil
Fresh corn-basil soup, 52
Gin-basil smash, 27
Green sauce–marinated shrimp, 91
Quick-cook fresh tomato sauce, 146
Stir-fried tofu with scallions, 115
Bean thread noodles, xii

Beef
Coffee and chili-crusted tenderloin, 107
Hoisin-marinated London broil, 103
Roast beef and Napa cabbage slaw, 64

Beverages
Coconut-cucumber splash, 31
Gin-basil smash, 27
Lotsa fruit spritzers, 32
Mango-coconut agua fresca, 29
Watermelon mojitos, 28

Black bean–corn salsa
South-of-the-border salad, 71

Black beans
Chilaquiles bake, 16

Black bean sauce
Chicken with black bean sauce, 94

Blood oranges
Double orange–mint salad, 75

Blueberries
Red, white, and blue parfaits, 23

Bok choy
Miso-glazed salmon, 84
Braised Italian-style pork chops, 108
Braised red cabbage and pears, 125

Breakfast
Bacon and cheddar–coddled eggs, 13
Baked eggs in tomatoes Florentine, 8
Broccoli-egg strudel, 5
Cheddar grits with bacon and kale, 14
Chilaquiles bake, 16
Greek-style breakfast pitas, 11
Gruyère and asparagus frittata, 3
Maple breakfast pudding, 20
Overstuffed Western omelette, 4
Polenta with brown-sugar ricotta, 21

Red, white, and blue parfaits, 23
Savory spinach-Parmesan oats, 174
Savory steel-cut oats with kale, 17
Skinny breakfast sausages and eggs, 12
Tropical oats with chia seeds, 18
Zucchini and goat cheese omelette, 7

Broccoli
Broccoli-egg strudel, 5
Chickpea-broccoli soup, 63
Sesame broccoli, 124

Bruschetta
Edamame-tomato bruschetta, 40

Brussels sprouts
Roasted Brussels sprouts with walnuts, 122

Bulgur
Spicy bulgur with carrots and harissa, 158

Burgers
Fresh salmon-ginger burgers, 82
Spicy blue cheese–chicken burgers, 95
Butterflied lamb with couscous salad, 112

Butternut squash
Warm roasted butternut squash salad, 68

C

Cabbage
Braised red cabbage and pears, 125
Roast beef and Napa cabbage slaw, 64

Canadian bacon
Cheddar grits with bacon and kale, 14

Cardamom
Coconut-cardamom basmati rice, 180

Carrots
Carrot-horseradish puree, 128
Root vegetable chips, 44
Spicy bulgur with carrots

and harissa, 158
Very French grated carrot salad, 127
Cast-iron skillet potato kugel, 166

Catfish
Catfish with salsa and olives, 88

Cauliflower
Cauliflower with lemon and cumin, 129
Whole roasted tandoori cauliflower, 131

Cheddar cheese
Bacon and cheddar–coddled eggs, 13
Cheddar potato "fries," 167
Cheddar grits with bacon and kale, 14
Cheddar potato "fries," 167
Cheese. *See* Cheddar cheese; feta cheese; goat cheese; Gorgonzola cheese; Gruyère cheese; Jarlsberg cheese; mozzarella cheese; Parmesan cheese; Pecorino-Romano cheese; PepperJack cheese; ricotta cheese; swiss cheese
Cheesy kale crisps, 45

Cherries
Cherry and thyme–stuffed pork, 110

Cherry tomatoes
Tomato and garlic–stuffed peppers, 144

Chia seeds
Red, white, and blue parfaits, 23
Tropical oats with chia seeds, 18

Chicken
Chicken kebabs with pineapple, 97
Chicken with black bean sauce, 94
Pecan-crusted buttermilk chicken, 92
Spicy blue cheese–chicken burgers, 95

Chickpea flour, xii
Silky chickpea soup with cumin, 50

Chickpeas
Chickpea-broccoli soup, 63
Couscous with chickpeas

and oranges, 162
Sumac-dusted onion and chickpeas, 78
Chilaquiles bake, 16
Chili-garlic sauce, xii
Chili oil, xii
Chocolate-orange mousse, 189
Chunky cucumber-yogurt salad, 72
Chunky guacamole-topped rice cakes, 34
Classic French potato salad, 172

Coconut
Coconut-cumin green beans, 135
Coconut-cardamom basmati rice, 180

Coconut chips
Tropical oats with chia seeds, 18
Coconut-cucumber splash, 31
Coconut-cumin green beans, 135
Coconut-curry tomato soup, 62

Coconut milk
Coconut-cardamom basmati rice, 180
Coconut-curry tomato soup, 62
Coconut oil, xii

Coconut water
Coconut-cucumber splash, 31
Mango-coconut agua fresca, 29
Tropical oats with chia seeds, 18
Coffee and chili-crusted tenderloin, 107

Coleslaw mix
Reuben-style quesadillas, 41

Corn
"Creamed" corn, 134
Fresh corn-basil soup, 52
Grilled Parmesan corn on the cob, 132

Couscous
Butterflied lamb with couscous salad, 112
Couscous with chickpeas and oranges, 162
Crab salad–topped cucumber, 36

Cranberries
Maple breakfast pudding, 20
"Creamed" corn, 134

Crème fraîche, xii
Crispy Hasselback potatoes, 165
Cucumbers. *See also* English
  cucumber
    Chunky cucumber-yogurt
      salad, 72
    Coconut-cucumber splash, 31
Currants
    Mixed rice pilaf with
      orange, 182
Curried barley with apricots, 152

D

Desserts
    Baked almond crisp–topped
      peaches, 188
    Banana–chocolate chip
      "ice cream," 193
    Chocolate-orange mousse, 189
    Hibiscus granita with grilled
      mango, 197
    Matcha-chocolate meringue
      bark, 192
    Plum crostata, 187
    Red wine–poached pears, 190
    Vanilla-bean panna cotta, 195
Dips
    Greek tzatziki dip, 37
Double orange–mint salad, 75

E

Edamame
    Edamame-tomato
      bruschetta, 40
    Seared scallops with
      edamame puree, 89
Eggplant
    Three-vegetable tian, 149
Eggs
    Bacon and cheddar–coddled
      eggs, 13
    Baked eggs in tomatoes
      Florentine, 8
    Broccoli-egg strudel, 5
    Cast-iron skillet potato
      kugel, 166
    Chilaquiles bake, 16
    Greek-style breakfast pitas, 11
    Gruyère and asparagus
      frittata, 3

Matcha-chocolate meringue
  bark, 192
Mustardy deviled eggs, 33
Overstuffed Western
  omelette, 4
Parmesan-pepper green
  bean "fries," 43
The real deal fried rice, 178
Skinny breakfast sausage
  and eggs, 12
Thai egg drop soup, 61
Zucchini and goat cheese
  omelette, 7
English cucumber. *See also*
  cucumbers
    Crab salad–topped
      cucumber, 36
    Greek tzatziki dip, 37

F

Fennel
    Lemony fennel and
      radicchio, 137
Feta cheese
    Greek-style breakfast pitas, 11
    Grilled zucchini with feta
      and lemon, 147
    Red quinoa salad with
      oranges, 76
Fermented black beans, xii
Fish and seafood
    Baked tilapia with grapes
      and olives, 85
    Catfish with salsa and
      olives, 88
    Crab salad–topped
      cucumber, 36
    Flounder in crazy water, 87
    Fresh salmon-ginger
      burgers, 82
    Green sauce–marinated
      shrimp, 91
    Miso-glazed salmon, 84
    Niçoise-inspired tuna
      salad, 67
    Pea soup with smoked
      salmon, 59
    Seared scallops with
      edamame puree, 89
Fish sauce, xii
Flounder in crazy water, 87

Freezer, ingredients in, xi
Fresh corn-basil soup, 52
Fresh pea salad with bacon, 74
Fresh salmon-ginger
  burgers, 82
Fridge, ingredients in, xi
Frittata
    Gruyère and asparagus
      frittata, 3
Fruit spreads
    Cherry and thyme–stuffed
      pork, 110
    Turkey fingers with peach
      sauce, 98

G

Garam masala, xiii
German-style potato-
  sauerkraut salad, 168
Gin-basil smash, 27
Goat cheese
    Grilled turkey saltimbocca, 101
    Warm roasted butternut
      squash salad, 68
    Zucchini and goat cheese
      omelette, 7
Gorgonzola cheese
    Greens with Gorgonzola and
      almonds, 65
Granola
    Red, white, and blue
      parfaits, 23
Grapes
    Baked tilapia with grapes
      and olives, 85
Grape tomatoes
    South-of-the-border salad, 71
    White beans with roasted
      tomatoes, 157
Greek-style breakfast pitas, 11
Greek tzatziki dip, 37
Greek yogurt. *See also* yogurt
    Greek tzatziki dip, 37
Green beans
    Coconut-cumin green
      beans, 135
    Parmesan-pepper green
      bean "fries," 43
Green bell peppers
    Braised Italian-style pork
      chops, 108

Overstuffed Western omelette, 4

Greens with Gorgonzola and almonds, 65

Grilled Parmesan corn on the cob, 132

Grilled zucchini with feta and lemon, 147

Grits
  Cheddar grits with bacon and kale, 14
  Gruyère and asparagus frittata, 3

H

Ham. *See also* pork
  Overstuffed Western omelette, 4
  The real deal fried rice, 178

Harissa, xiii

Hibiscus granita with grilled mango, 197

Hoisin-marinated London broil, 103

Hoisin sauce, xii

Horseradish, xiii

Hot and smoky pink beans, 155

I

Ingredients
  In pantry, fridge, and freezer, xi

J

Jalapeño peppers
  Chicken kebabs with pineapple, 97
  Chunky guacamole–topped rice cakes, 34

Jarlsberg cheese
  Broccoli-egg strudel, 5

Jicama
  South-of-the-border salad, 71

K

Kale
  Cheddar grits with bacon and kale, 14
  Cheesy kale crisps, 45
  Savory steel-cut oats with kale, 17

Warm roasted butternut squash salad, 68

Kebabs
  Chicken kebabs with pineapple, 97

Kecap manis, xii

Kimchee, xii

L

Lamb
  Butterflied lamb with couscous salad, 112

Leeks
  Simple potato-leek soup, 60

Lemon
  Cauliflower with lemon and cumin, 129
  Grilled zucchini with feta and lemon, 147
  Lemon and pecorino popcorn, 47
  Lemon barley, 154
  Lemony fennel and radicchio, 137

Lemongrass, xiii

Lentils
  Kielbasa and lentil stew, 104
  North African red lentil soup, 54

Lima beans
  Stir-fried tofu with scallions, 115

Lotsa fruit spritzers, 32

M

Mangoes
  Hibiscus granita with grilled mango, 197
  Mango-coconut agua fresca, 29

Maple breakfast pudding, 20

Marinated tofu and vegetable kebabs, 119

Mascarpone, xiii

Mashed parsnips, potatoes, and apple, 163

Matcha-chocolate meringue bark, 192

Milk. *See* soy milk

Mint
  Double orange–mint salad, 75
  Sumac-dusted onion and

chickpeas, 78

Watermelon mojitos, 28

Mirin, xiii

Miso, xiii
  Miso-glazed salmon, 84
  Miso soup with tofu and scallions, 53
  Soba noodle–mushroom soup, 57

Mozzarella cheese
  Grilled Swiss chard and tomato pizzas, 109
  Polenta "pizza" margherita, 116
  Romaine and sun-dried tomato salad, 70

Mushrooms
  Hearty turkey-barley stew, 102
  Miso soup with tofu and scallions, 53
  Soba noodle–mushroom soup, 57

Mustardy deviled eggs, 33

N

Naan, xiv

Niçoise-inspired tuna salad, 67

North African red lentil soup, 54

Nuts. *See* almonds; pistachios; walnuts

O

Oats
  Baked almond crisp–topped peaches, 188
  Savory spinach-Parmesan oats, 174
  Savory steel-cut oats with kale, 17
  Tropical oats with chia seeds, 18

Olives
  Baked tilapia with grapes and olives, 85
  Catfish with salsa and olives, 88
  Niçoise-inspired tuna salad, 67
  Provençal tomato tart, 38

Omelettes
  Overstuffed Western omelette, 4

Zucchini and goat cheese omelette, 7

Oranges
Chocolate-orange mousse, 189
Couscous with chickpeas and oranges, 162
Double orange–mint salad, 75
Mixed rice pilaf with orange, 182
Red quinoa salad with oranges, 76
Overstuffed Western omelette, 4
Oyster sauce, xiv

P

Pancetta, xiv
Pantry, ingredients in, xi
Parfaits
Red, white, and blue parfaits, 23
Parmesan cheese
Baked eggs in tomatoes Florentine, 8
Chickpea-broccoli soup, 63
Grilled Parmesan corn on the cob, 132
Parmesan-pepper green bean "fries," 43
Polenta "pizza" margherita, 116
Polenta with spinach and cheese, 177
Provençal tomato tart, 38
Roasted garlic-herb bread, 181
Savory spinach-Parmesan oats, 174
Parmigiano-Reggiano, xiv
Parsnips
Mashed parsnips, potatoes, and apple, 163
Root vegetable chips, 44
Peaches
Baked almond crisp–topped peaches, 188
Pears
Braised red cabbage and pears, 125
Red wine–poached pears, 190
Peas
Fresh pea salad with bacon, 74
Pea soup with smoked

salmon, 59
Peas with crispy prosciutto, 139
Spicy bulgur with carrots and harissa, 158
Pecan-crusted buttermilk chicken, 92
Pecorino-Romano cheese
Cheesy kale crisps, 45
Lemon and pecorino popcorn, 47
Pecorino-Romano, xiv
Pepper jack cheese
Chilaquiles bake, 16
Peppers. *See* green bell peppers; jalapeño peppers; red bell peppers; sweet peppers
Pepperoncini, xiv
Phyllo dough
Broccoli-egg strudel, 5
Provençal tomato tart, 38
Pineapple
Chicken kebabs with pineapple, 97
Tropical oats with chia seeds, 18
Pine nuts
Red quinoa with parsley and pine nuts, 175
Pink beans
Hot and smoky pink beans, 155
Pistachios
Curried barley with apricots, 152
Pizza
Grilled Swiss chard and tomato pizzas, 109
Polenta "pizza" margherita, 116
Plum crostata, 187
Plum tomatoes
Chunky guacamole-topped rice cakes, 34
Grilled Swiss chard and tomato pizzas, 109
Polenta "pizza" margherita, 116
Provençal tomato tart, 38
Three-vegetable tian, 149
Poblano chile
South-of-the-border salad, 71
Polenta
Polenta "pizza" margherita, 116
Polenta with brown-sugar ricotta, 21

Polenta with spinach and cheese, 177
Popcorn
Lemon and pecorino popcorn, 47
Pork. *See also* ham
Braised Italian-style pork chops, 108
Cherry and thyme–stuffed pork, 110
Potatoes
Cheddar potato "fries," 167
Classic French potato salad, 172
Crispy Hasselback potatoes, 165
German-style potato-sauerkraut salad, 168
Mashed parsnips, potatoes, and apple, 163
Pea soup with smoked salmon, 59
Simple potato-leek soup, 60
Smashed potatoes with lemon salt, 171
Prosciutto, xiv
Grilled turkey saltimbocca, 101
Peas with crispy prosciutto, 139
Provençal tomato tart, 38

Q

Quesadillas
Reuben-style quesadillas, 41
Quick-cook fresh tomato sauce, 146
Quinoa
Red quinoa salad with oranges, 76
Red quinoa with parsley and pine nuts, 175

R

Radicchio
Lemony fennel and radicchio, 137
Warm roasted butternut squash salad, 68
Radishes
Rosemary-roasted radishes, 141

Raisins
  Maple breakfast pudding, 20
Raspberries
  Red, white, and blue parfaits, 23
Red bell peppers
  Braised Italian-style pork
    chops, 108
  Marinated tofu and
    vegetable kebabs, 119
  Overstuffed Western
    omelette, 4
  Tomato and garlic–stuffed
    peppers, 144
Red quinoa salad with
  oranges, 76
Red quinoa with parsley and
  pine nuts, 175
Red, white, and blue parfaits, 23
Red wine–poached pears, 190
Reuben-style quesadillas, 41
Rice
  Coconut-cardamom basmati
    rice, 180
  Maple breakfast pudding, 20
  Mixed rice pilaf with
    orange, 182
  The real deal fried rice, 178
Rice cakes
  Chunky guacamole-topped
    rice cakes, 34
Rice stick noodles, xiv
Ricotta cheese
  Polenta "pizza" margherita, 116
  Polenta with brown-sugar
    ricotta, 21
Ricotta salata, xiv
Roast beef and Napa cabbage
  slaw, 64
Roasted acorn squash with thyme,
  143
Roasted garlic-herb bread, 181
Romaine lettuce
  Romaine and sun-dried
    tomato salad, 70
  South-of-the-border salad, 71
Root vegetable chips, 44
Rosemary-roasted radishes, 141

S

Salad dressings. *See also*
  vinaigrettes

Reuben-style quesadillas, 41
Roast beef and Napa
  cabbage slaw, 64
Spicy blue cheese–chicken
  burgers, 95
Salads
  Butterflied lamb with
    couscous salad, 112
  Chunky cucumber-yogurt
    salad, 72
  Classic French potato salad, 172
  Double orange–mint salad, 75
  Fresh pea salad with bacon, 74
  Greens with Gorgonzola and
    almonds, 65
  Niçoise-inspired tuna salad, 67
  Red quinoa salad with
    oranges, 76
  Romaine and sun-dried
    tomato salad, 70
  South-of-the-border salad, 71
  Sumac-dusted onion and
    chickpeas, 78
  Very French grated carrot
    salad, 127
  Warm roasted butternut
    squash salad, 69
Salmon
  Fresh salmon-ginger
    burgers, 82
  Miso-glazed salmon, 84
  Pea soup with smoked
    salmon, 59
Salsa
  Catfish with salsa and
    olives, 88
  Chilaquiles bake, 16
Sambal oelek, xiv
Sandwich bread
  Fresh salmon-ginger
    burgers, 82
Sauerkraut
  German-style potato-
    sauerkraut salad, 168
Savory spinach-Parmesan
  oats, 174
Savory steel-cut oats with kale, 17
Scallions
  Curried barley with
    apricots, 152
  Miso soup with tofu and
    scallions, 53

The real deal fried rice, 178
Stir-fried tofu with scallions, 115
Scallops
  Seared scallops with
    edamame puree, 89
Seeds. *See* chia seeds
Seltzer
  Lotsa fruit spritzers, 32
Sesame broccoli, 124
Sesame seeds
  Matcha-chocolate meringue
    bark, 192
  Sesame broccoli, 124
Shrimp
  Green sauce–marinated
    shrimp, 91
Silky chickpea soup with
  cumin, 50
Simple potato-leek soup, 60
Skinny breakfast sausages
  and eggs, 12
Slaw
  Roast beef and Napa
    cabbage slaw, 64
Smashed potatoes with
  lemon salt, 171
Soba noodle–mushroom soup, 57
Soups
  Chickpea-broccoli soup, 63
  Coconut-curry tomato soup, 62
  Fresh corn-basil soup, 52
  Miso soup with tofu and
    scallions, 53
  North African red lentil soup, 54
  Pea soup with smoked
    salmon, 59
  Silky chickpea soup with
    cumin, 50
  Simple potato-leek soup, 60
  Soba noodle–mushroom
    soup, 57
  Thai egg drop soup, 61
South-of-the-border salad, 71
Spaghettini
  Stir-fried tofu with scallions, 115
Spicy blue cheese–chicken
  burgers, 95
Spicy bulgur with carrots and
  harissa, 158
Spinach
  Bacon and cheddar–
    coddled eggs, 13

Baked eggs in tomatoes Florentine, 8
Greek-style breakfast pitas, 11
Polenta with spinach and cheese, 177
Savory spinach-Parmesan oats, 174
Soba noodle–mushroom soup, 57
Stir-fried garlic spinach, 142
Sriracha, xiii

Stew
Hearty turkey-barley stew, 102
Kielbasa and lentil stew, 104
Stir-fried garlic spinach, 142
Stir-fried tofu with scallions, 115

Strawberries
Lotsa fruit spritzers, 32
Red, white, and blue parfaits, 23

Sumac, xiii
Sumac-dusted onion and chickpeas, 78

Sun-dried tomatoes
Romaine and sun-dried tomato salad, 70

Sweet peppers
The real deal fried rice, 178

Sweet potatoes
Root vegetable chips, 44

Swiss chard
Grilled Swiss chard and tomato pizzas, 109

Swiss cheese
Reuben-style quesadillas, 41

T

Tarts
Provençal tomato tart, 38
Thai curry paste, xiv
Thai egg drop soup, 61
Three-vegetable tian, 149

Tilapia
Baked tilapia with grapes and olives, 85

Tofu
Marinated tofu and vegetable kebabs, 119
Miso soup with tofu and scallions, 53

Stir-fried tofu with scallions, 115
Tomato and garlic–stuffed peppers, 144

Tomatoes. *See* cherry tomatoes; grape tomatoes; plum tomatoes; sun-dried tomatoes
Baked eggs in tomatoes Florentine, 8
Butterflied lamb with couscous salad, 112
Chickpea-broccoli soup, 63
Coconut-curry tomato soup, 62
Edamame-tomato bruschetta, 40
Flounder in crazy water, 87
Kielbasa and lentil stew, 104
Niçoise-inspired tuna salad, 67
North African red lentil soup, 54
Provençal tomato tart, 38
Quick-cook fresh tomato sauce, 146
Stir-fried tofu with scallions, 115

Tomato sauce
Braised Italian-style pork chops, 108

Tortillas
Chilaquiles bake, 16
Reuben-style quesadillas, 41
Tropical oats with chia seeds, 18

Tuna
Niçoise-inspired tuna salad, 67

Turkey
German-style potato-sauerkraut salad, 168
Grilled turkey saltimbocca, 101
Hearty turkey-barley stew, 102
Kielbasa and lentil stew, 104
Pan-glazed turkey tenderloin, 99
Reuben-style quesadillas, 41
Skinny breakfast sausage and eggs, 12
Turkey fingers with peach sauce, 98

Turkey bacon
Savory steel-cut oats with kale, 17

V

Vadouvan, xiii
Vanilla-bean panna cotta, 195

Vegetable broth
Fresh corn-basil soup, 52

W

Walnuts
Roasted Brussels sprouts with walnuts, 122
Warm roasted butternut squash salad, 68
Warm roasted butternut squash salad, 69
Watermelon mojitos, 28
White beans with roasted tomatoes, 157

Whole grains
Cooking, 161
Tips and tricks with, 160
Whole roasted tandoori cauliflower, 131

Y

Yogurt. *See also* Greek yogurt
Chocolate-orange mousse, 189
Chunky cucumber-yogurt salad, 72
North African red lentil soup, 54
Red, white, and blue parfaits, 23

Z

Zucchini
Grilled zucchini with feta and lemon, 147
Lemon barley, 154
Marinated tofu and vegetable kebabs, 119
Three-vegetable tian, 149
Zucchini and goat cheese omelette, 7

FOI

DEC 0 2 2024